On High Lakeland Fells

Over 120 of the Best Walks and Scrambles

On High Lakeland Fells

Over 120 of the Best Walks and Scrambles

Bob Allen

FRANCES LINCOLN

Frances Lincoln Ltd
4 Torriano Mews
Torriano Avenue
London NW5 2RZ
www.franceslincoln.com

On High Lakeland Fells
Text copyright © Bob Allen 1987, 2005
Photographs copyright © Bob Allen
Maps © Bob Allen 1987, 2005

First published by Pic Limited, Glossop, 1987
This revised edition published by Frances Lincoln Ltd, 2005

A catalogue record for this book is available from
the British Library.

ISBN 0 7112 2527 3

Printed and bound in Singapore

9 8 7 6 5 4 3 2 1

Right: From Sail to the Dodds Ridge
Front cover: Lingmell from near Calf Cove, Scafell Pike.
Back cover: Middle Dodd from Red Screes with Ullswater beyond.
Previous page: Bowfell from Earring Crag

CONTENTS

INTRODUCTION

After several reprints in its original form, this book has been completely revised and updated, with nearly fifty new colour photographs and clearer maps with more information. It describes more than 120 of the best walks and scrambles on the high peaks and ridges of the English Lake District. The lower and lowest fells are covered in two separate books: *On Lower Lakeland Fells* and *Short Walks in the Lake District*. However, it aims to provide many other suggestions as well.

THE WALKS

Of the eighty-four walks covered, seventy-three of them are 'rounds' enabling an easy return to be made to the starting point at the end of the day. In eleven cases, however, the routes are traverses, thus making it vital to have backup transport to complete the outing.

The walks are rated by a star system to indicate overall quality, with three stars indicating the best routes, in my opinion. Fine mountain scenery, good situations and continuous interest (or lack of it) are all factors to be included when considering the quality of a walk. It is a subjective assessment but one which still seems to command general agreement. Lack of stars does not necessarily mean that a particular walk is not worth doing, but the use of this system may be helpful to a newcomer to a particular part of the district. The walks are not rambles or strolls, since they are over the high ground and require – including reasonable stops – from four hours walking time up to twelve hours in the case of a very few 'marathon walks'.

Approximate times: These are given at the beginning of each chapter and are just that, approximate. I have not altered them for this edition; they were originally set when I was personally fitter than I am now, nearly twenty years later. If you add twenty per cent to them you should be all right. They do allow for a (quick) stop for lunch and assume that the party will be reasonably fit. Naismith's Rule, allowing one hour for every three miles, plus an additional thirty minutes per thousand feet (c.300 metres) of ascent, is a reasonable guide, though in my experience most parties do more stopping than Naismith allows for.

Maps: The book is divided into thirteen sections each representing a reasonably well-defined geographical area and, with the exception of Black Combe, all the highest points of land inside the Lake District are included. Although I have drawn separate sketch maps for each chapter they are only sketches intended to point out the general line of a walk or scramble. For more detail Harveys or Ordnance Survey maps are needed, especially when it comes to escaping from the confines of the intake walls to get to the high fells. I assume that all fell-walkers know how to use a magnetic compass in conjunction with them. English 1:40,000, 1:50,000 and 1:25,000 scale tourist maps are superb.

THE SCRAMBLES

About fifty-five scrambles are described or indicated. The best of them are very enjoyable in their own right and many of them are close by recognised footpaths, thus providing more adventurous ways to the fell-tops. The whole art of scrambling consists of linking together solid bits of rock in the most continuously interesting line, either up the course of a stream or up a mountain-side. Of course scrambling at times deteriorates into 'scramble-walking' up scree, grass and other vegetation and there is almost always an easier way to be found than any particular one described here, though with loss of interest and sense of adventure. The lines of demarcation between rambling and fell-walking, scrambling and rock-climbing are blurred, but I understand 'scrambling' to be a combination of fell-walking with rock-climbing at its very easiest.

Star rating for the scrambles: This is the same as that used for the walks, the aim being to give an overall indication of their quality.

Grading of difficulty for the scrambles: Here I have used a numerical grading system, with 3 as the hardest grade and 1 as the easiest. Grade 1 scrambles will involve the occasional use of the hands on steep ground (e.g. Jack's Rake on Pavey Ark or Sharp Edge on Blencathra. (Both of these become harder in the wet!) Grade 2 will have individual passages which are a bit harder and a short rope MAY be useful to protect inexperienced members of a party. Grade 3 scrambling is that verging on the lowest grades of rock-climbing and could well include passages of 'Moderate' or 'Difficult' standard. It is advisable that at least

one member of a party should have some rock-climbing experience for Grade 2 and 3 scrambles to enjoy the best bits of rock and not to have to avoid all the most entertaining passages. The scrambling grades assume dry rock, not too much wind (or too much water in the gills) and air temperatures that allow the use of bare hands. Adverse weather conditions can transform an easy scramble into something very much more difficult. Only judgement based on experience can tell you when it is advisable to stick to the straightforward walk and leave the scramble for a better day. A torrential downpour on ice-coated rock, which may entertain an expert, is not 'normal'! If you choose to go on to a Grade 3 scramble under adverse conditions be sure that you have first learnt how to deal with some easier routes under similar conditions.

CLOTHING AND EQUIPMENT

Proper clothing is important because Lakeland weather (or almost all mountain weather) is rarely predictable for more than a few hours ahead and wetness and wind can be a lethal combination. Recent years have seen major developments in clothing, mostly using man-made fibres and marketed in a bewildering choice of fabrics and brands. Compared to traditional cotton or wool, these new fabrics are generally lighter in weight, less absorbent of water and therefore dry quicker. They are especially useful in situations of high exertion, where heavy perspiration is normal. Breathable fabrics (the original was Goretex but there are now many competitors), when used for outer shell garments, perform better when the layers of clothing beneath them are also of man-made fabrics.

Natural materials, however, still have their place. They can feel more comfortable and their absorbent qualities can be of benefit. For example, wool absorbs up to 20 per cent of its own weight of water and also naturally generates heat when wet. For gloves or socks these properties can be major benefits. The weather, or expected weather conditions, is all-important.

The choice of footwear has, nowadays, become almost equally bewildering. For general winter conditions, the traditional leather boot, reasonably stiffened and with a Vibram-type moulded rubber sole, is probably still the best. It needs to fit well and give good ankle support. But there are now waterproof-membrane boots with fabric uppers, which will do the job in most winter conditions, except the worst. All boots, leather or fabric, let the water in

eventually and it pays to have different boots for different conditions. That is, presumably, progress – and it keeps the economy growing.

A rucksack is virtually a necessity to carry spare clothes, waterproofs, food and liquids. I personally prefer the one that is slightly larger than generally recommended, as it sits easier on my back, e.g. a 40-litre to a 30-litre, but this is very much a personal matter. The use of telescopic walking poles has become very widespread of recent years as they can take a lot of weight off hip and knee joints and aid balance and stability on rough ground or in gusty weather. Two are definitely preferable to one. Don't worry about your image – nearly everybody has them nowadays.

Where there is ice about – and simple fell-walking becomes winter mountaineering – a long-handled ice-axe is more useful than the short technical axes, but the knowledge of how to use an axe for self-arrest in the event of a slip on high-angled icy ground is a necessity, while crampons may be essential. This is when the real enthusiasts come into their own, for our hills acquire even greater beauty, excitement and exhilaration at such times.

ACCESS AND ACCOMMODATION

The Lake District of the British Isles hardly needs a definition since it was 'discovered' by those eighteenth- and nineteenth-century poets, writers and painters who celebrated its marvellous natural scenery so superbly. The arrival of the railway at Windermere saw a further step forward in putting the Lake District 'on the map', but nowadays the M6 motorway, the Kendal bypass and the A66 trunk road from the M6 near Penrith through Keswick form the main highways into what is now the Lake District National Park. Fortunately the physical structure of the region means that there are very few routes, other than bridleways, from one side to the other. It is to be hoped that carefully implemented conservation policies will retain this unique part of the British Isles.

For accommodation the choice is almost endless, from the finest quality hotels and restaurants to pubs and family hotels, bed-and-breakfast accommodation, self-catering chalets, climbing-club huts for the use of their members and guests, Youth Hostels, caravan and camping sites – though the choice for touring caravans is very limited indeed within the main Lake District area. If in doubt as to where to stay probably the best advice is to arrive early enough to enquire and look around.

Haystacks and bluebells.

WORD SPELLINGS AND PLACE NAMES

There are problems over certain words which are used extensively in the Lake District and with two in particular: combe and gill. The word 'combe', meaning the hollow scooped by ice and water between retaining ridges, is often spelt as 'comb' and sometimes 'coomb'. I have used the spelling shown on the maps where it occurs, but have elsewhere used the spelling 'combe'. Most of the Lakeland watercourses down the fellsides are 'gills', though some are 'ghylls'. Again, I have used the map spelling where there is one, but in other places have used 'gill' – except where use and custom seem to dictate otherwise, as in Deep Ghyll or Moss Ghyll on Scafell for instance. One word that seems an oddity to me is the map spelling of what I have always known as 'Greta Gill', also on Scafell, where the map has 'Girta'. Perhaps wrongly, I have retained 'Greta'.

PHOTOGRAPHS

I hope that my new selection of photographs will give pleasure and inspiration. Just in case global warming means less snow I have retained many of my best winter photographs of the high fells for this edition.

ACKNOWLEDGMENTS

I should like to thank many friends who have, sometimes unknowingly but always without complaint, helped me in the preparation of this book. Geoff Milburn and his father Ken helped me greatly in the preparation of the first edition, as did Peter Hodgkiss and A. K. Carnegie. The late Trevor Jones, Diana McIlreavy, Roger Salisbury, Derek Walker, Roger Bowers, Jill Aldersley, Trevor Waller, Reg Atkins, various friends of the Fell and Rock Climbing Club and others – to whom I apologise if I can't recall their names at this moment – all came with me on walks and scrambles when I needed to check information or try to get some more photographs. Harry Griffin has been a particular source of inspiration and I was led to do much mountain exploring from his writings. Brian Evans' books on Lakeland scrambles were very useful as a check on my own explorations and as a source of further ideas.

My wife, Lin, put up with three years of my departing in the early hours and returning at very late ones when I wrote the original text and has now put up with something similar as I have revised and updated it. Finally, may I thank all those with whom I have shared the fellowship of the hills over the years and particularly the hill-walkers whose love of our unique Lakeland mountains first awoke my own interest.

The Langdale Pikes from near Chapel Stile.

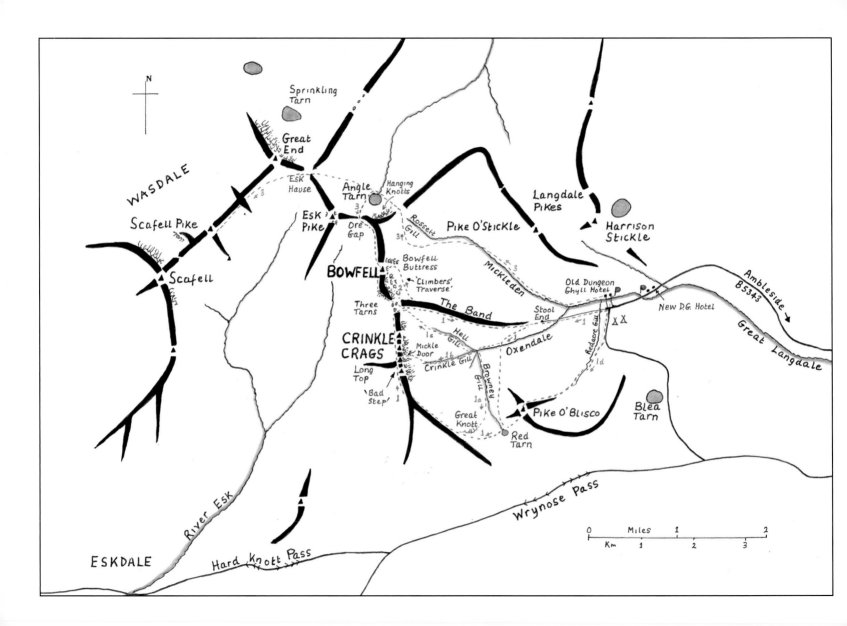

BOWFELL and CRINKLE CRAGS

	Approximate Time	Star Rating	Assessment of Difficulty
1. The Crinkle Crags Traverse	5–6 hours	***	—
Alternative starts via: 1a. Scramble in Browney Gill	add 1 hour	*	1–2
1b. Scramble in Crinkle Gill	add 1 hour	*	1–2
1c. Scramble in Hell Gill	add 1/2 hour	*	1–2
1d. Pike o' Blisco	add 1–11/2 hours	*	—
2. Bowfell by the Climbers' Traverse	5–6 hours	***	—
3. Bowfell or Scafell Pike via Rossett Gill	5–6 hours		—

BOWFELL and CRINKLE CRAGS

When William Wordsworth proposed that his reader place himself in imagination on a cloud midway between Great Gable and Scafell in order to see the valleys radiating like the spokes of a wheel from that vantage, he could equally have chosen Esk Hause, or possibly Bowfell, as the hub. As you may imagine, therefore, there are a lot of possible valley and ridge approaches to Bowfell, including the northern ones over Esk Hause. Bowfell and the Crinkles are however inescapably part of the great Langdale skyline and all the most dramatic crags are those that look down into Mickleden and Oxendale at the head of Langdale.

1. The Crinkle Crags Traverse

The Crinkles don't look anything special from the head of Langdale, merely a few knobbles on the skyline; but that is an illusion, for this traverse gives one of the roughest and rockiest walks in the Lake District, and it is a justifiably popular expedition. It can be done in either direction, but I have chosen the clockwise route as most people generally find it easier to climb up the little 'bad step' on No. 2 Crinkle rather than to descend it.

The normal starting point is the head of Great Langdale, from the Old Dungeon Ghyll Hotel (or, with a little longer walk, from the car park by the New Dungeon Ghyll Hotel), then take the farm track to Stool End Farm, which is the last one up the valley. This is at the foot of The Band, the long ridge descending from Bowfell, and there is an obvious track up it. Avoid this, however, and bear left along the valley floor, over a couple of stiles and up into Oxendale. The Crinkle Crags skyline looms distantly but directly ahead and paths lead towards it; but bear left again (south) over the very bouldery stream bed to a footbridge. A partially 'pitched' path up a sometimes boggy slope ahead climbs steadily, then skirts the left bank of Browney Gill, rising to reach the level ground between Pike o' Blisco and Cold Pike, where Red Tarn lies in a reedy bed. (Incidentally, thinking to gain some initial height by mechanical means, walkers are regularly tempted to reach Red Tarn by leaving transport at Wrynose Pass – from Little Langdale to the Duddon Valley – but the idea is less attractive when they are faced with an uphill walk at the end of the day.)

From Red Tarn a rising path traverses the fellside of Cold Pike, just west of the rocky bluff of Great Knott, and on to a sloping plateau of stones and peaty ground which seems to go on interminably. However, this ends rather suddenly and the Crinkles are within reach at last – up a little stone-shoot on to the rough rocks of the First Crinkle, where the way is well-cairned and obvious. Beyond the First Crinkle there is a drop into a shallow depression and the path enters a gully choked by a couple of big boulders, with no immediately obvious exit. There is no doubt that this sudden obstacle causes palpitations in the breasts of many walkers reaching this point, especially when doing the traverse anti-clockwise, but a couple of obvious and well-used holds on the right-hand wall lead immediately to easier ground.

However, there are two alternatives. The first is to go left before you enter the gully and follow a rocky, grooved staircase more or less on the corner of the steep rocks, which requires only minimal use of the hands, but is a little exposed. This reaches a ledge traversing back to the normal way but above the difficulties. The second alternative is to walk much farther left below all the steep rocks until you can circle back without using hands at all, though in forty years I have never seen anybody actually finding this necessary.

Above this little 'bad step' the path leads up and over the Second Crinkle, which is the highest and biggest. It throws a distinct spur of rock westwards towards Eskdale, named Long Top and there is a faint path stretching along it – possibly made by walkers going out to look at the dramatic views over to the Scafell group. If the weather is at all misty it will pay to check your compass bearing regularly, for the line of the main ridge is south to north (in this direction) but the path that follows it twists and turns up and down in a confusing way. There are several variants to the main path and it is easy to go wrong in mist; too late you realise that you are descending into Eskdale instead of into Langdale.

At the end of the rocky descent from the Second Crinkle, the path crosses the head of the wide scree gully of 'Mickle Door', falling towards Langdale. It then avoids the summit of the Third Crinkle, which is a pity, for there are fine views down the ravines of Oxendale and to the green fields of Mickleden from its rocky top.

Bowfell rises ahead now, seen as a true and shapely mountain, with the seamed and eroded face of the Bowfell Links clearly in view, as the main path passes through a wilderness of stones just below the summits of the Fourth and Fifth Crinkles. Two separate tiny tarns are passed as the path leads over the shoulder of Shelter Crags then descends gently to the hause separating them from Bowfell. Finding the Three Tarns here is a good indication that you are not lost. Now, unless you choose to continue to Bowfell summit, the *fastest* descent is probably down the broad ridge of The Band. To use this, a well-defined path descends from the hause to the north-east, veering south-east to reach The Band. It will get you down to Stool End Farm in a good half hour or so. (If you trot, of course.)

It is softer underfoot and perhaps scenically more interesting to avoid The Band. Instead, turn eastwards down the slope on a fainter path and follow the infant beck downwards. A line of small cairns soon leads to a good path skirting the rocky edge of the dramatic Hell Gill. Although on one section the steepness of the descent would have you gallop along, it is soon over and the sound of rushing water pouring down the great ravine on the left enhances the splendid views to Pike o' Blisco, showing its distinctive shape to great advantage from here. On reaching the valley floor, after crossing a footbridge you regain your ascent route and can return home the richer for a splendid day on the hill.

Alternative starts via scrambles in Browney Gill, Crinkle Gill or Hell Gill

Three fine gills converge at the same point at the head of Oxendale and two of these provide very enjoyable alternative starts to the normal Crinkle Crags traverse described above. The third, Hell Gill, although dramatic, is more suitable as a start to the Crinkles Traverse in an anti-clockwise direction. Let us start with Browney Gill.

1a. Alternative start via Browney Gill

The starting point of all these gill scrambles is reached simply by walking a little farther up Oxendale from Stool End Farm than for the normal path up to Red Tarn. Don't cross the footbridge on the left amongst the chaos of boulders but continue a little farther up the right bank then, just after passing a rocky moraine 'castle', descend into the bed of Browney Gill, which is the left-hand prong of the trident. You are immediately confronted by a deep pool, but roots and a stout

The Summit of Pike o' Blisco, with Bowfell.

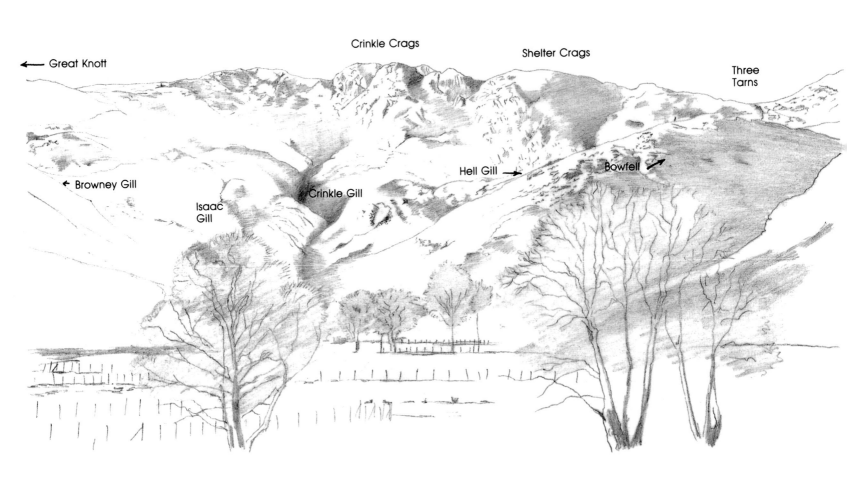

Great Knott

Crinkle Crags

Shelter Crags

Three Tarns

Browney Gill

Isaac Gill

Crinkle Gill

Hell Gill

Bowfell

branch from the tree overhanging it are usually enough to enable this obstacle to be overcome. Beyond there is a long stretch of bouldery ravine bed and no particular difficulty until the gorge becomes much narrower. At one point it is necessary to straddle across for a few moves until easier holds are reached on the right. Farther on, a small amphitheatre is reached, where the stream pours through a deep cleft, but the only risk is of wet feet and strategically-placed boulders should enable those to be avoided. A long open stretch leads to the point where the gill bends to the right and is without much interest, but it is easy to leave the bed of the gill and go left to join the main path heading for Red Tarn and so gain the usual track to the Crinkles.

It is, however, perfectly feasible to continue for quite a way in the upper gill and there are no particular problems until a series of much steeper cascades looms up ahead. These are climbable but the rock is not above suspicion and low water conditions are highly desirable. An alternative now to is to leave the bed of the gill for its right-hand side and strike up the fellside for a little way to reach the lower rocks of Great Knott, which are obvious ahead. They look and are fairly steep, but they provide a staircase of perfect rock with large and excellent holds for a hundred feet or more. The summit of Great Knott is then just a short walk away and you get a full view of the whole of the Crinkles Traverse laid out before your eyes.

1b. Alternative start via Crinkle Gill

This starts from the same place and is the central one of the three main gills. It is my own favourite because it enables me to miss out the most boring bits of the approach to the Crinkles ridge. On one long section the walls of the gill are quite high and very steep; modern rock-climbers have discovered them but, luckily, you are just walking up the rocks in the stream-bed. Fortunately it is all straightforward until you reach the amphitheatre, with up to four small streams pouring into it. Head for the right-hand side, scramble up an obvious sloping slab on to a narrow sort of neck, then follow a slim path leading easily out of the gill.

Above the amphitheatre work your way up the fellside towards two great buttresses that tower ahead – the right-hand one of which is more sharply pointed. Between them, visible as you gain height, is the big scree shoot of Mickle Door and a path of sorts wends its way up its left hand side to reach the ridge above. However, for scramblers with rock-climbing experience, there is an exhilarating long scramble up the rocks and terraces of the buttress on the right hand side of Mickle Door. At the time of writing this route has been little used and still has an air of exploration about it.

1c. Alternative start via Hell Gill

Hell Gill is not the most suitable place for the enjoyable sport of leaping from rock to rock doing your best to avoid wet feet, because there is no direct way out up the vertical waterfall of Whorneyside Force (except when it is frozen). However, it is an impressive place and its name seems appropriate enough when you are underneath its black and vegetated walls. It is the right-hand of the three gills (the one with a footbridge at its foot) and the start is easy enough, though after bypassing a small waterfall a large jammed boulder is a bit of an obstacle. Sadly, too soon after that you are in the final amphitheatre with its great cascade and wonderful pool. Now it is best to either reverse steps or exit leftwards by a somewhat precarious scramble to the fellside to reach the footpath above. Unlike the other two gills it is all over before it has hardly begun. The walk then continues to Three Tarns and then over the Crinkles, in an anti-clockwise direction.

1d. Variation start including Pike o' Blisco

Pike o' Blisco has a fine, stony summit (two summits, in fact) of delicate grey and pink rock, with good views, especially to Crinkle Crags and Bowfell. Many walkers rightly incorporate it in their circuit of the Crinkles. For this variation, instead of making for the foot of The Band, head up the road from Great Langdale towards Blea Tarn and Little Langdale, soon turning off to follow the path up Redacre Gill. It is a steep ascent, with a pitched path up the last part of the gill, but well worth the effort.

Pike o' Blisco is certainly engraved indelibly in my memory, for at fifteen years of age, on my first ever visit to the Lakes one Easter, a school friend and I camped behind the rhododendrons at the side of Blea Tarn. That night it snowed, and when we got up we were glad to get going because we were so cold. Shouldering huge rucksacks, packed with tent, sleeping bag, cooking gear, food for a week, spare clothes, etc., we headed straight up the very steep hillside behind Blea Tarn, heading west for Pike o' Blisco and beyond. There is no vestige of a track up there, nor ever likely to be as there is a lot of steep, wet and generally horrible rock and much vegetation. But at fifteen we were very determined and inexperienced and we pressed on upwards, with difficulty. Admittedly a few snow squalls didn't help our route-finding, but when we reached the summit of Blake Rigg we thought we were on the summit of Pike o' Blisco. So we carried on, heading, as we thought, for Bowfell, and when we reached Pike o' Blisco we thought we *had* reached Bowfell. We decided that the mountain group that we could then see ahead *must* be Scafell, so off we tramped – to Crinkle Crags! Traversing these in deep, wet snow with heavy packs proved a bit demoralising for my friend and he refused to climb to what we thought was Scafell Pike – but which was actually the summit of Bowfell. However, I was determined not to *lose* height, so we traversed the Langdale face of Bowfell by what must have been the Climbers' Traverse, except that beyond Bowfell Buttress we kept on traversing. Eventually we reached the head of Rossett Gill, but it wasn't till we caught sight of Angle Tarn that we really sorted out where we were. Incredible as it seems to me now, we then walked over Esk Hause, straight up and over Great Gable and down into the head of Ennerdale. We erected our tent that night on snow-sprinkled bog, a short distance from the tiny Youth Hostel and just outside the Forestry Commission fence. We slept like logs that night.

From Pike o' Blisco a cairned path descends the other side of the hill to Red Tarn, where the normal track for the Crinkles is joined.

BOWFELL

The normal way up Bowfell from Langdale is, of course, straight up the ridge of The Band, from Stool End Farm, to reach Three Tarns. Then, swinging north, a path up a wide gully leads to the summit of this shapely mountain. (This is also the obvious continuation to Bowfell from the Crinkle Crags traverse just described.)

To reach Bowfell from the west side, either from Eskdale or from Mosedale starting at Cockley Beck, the walk goes by the bank of the Lingcove Beck to the boggy ground called Green Hole, then up tedious slopes to Three Tarns – not an attractive ascent route in my opinion. Much more rewarding is a lesser-known, and not so obvious, way up and down Bowfell and that is the one that I will now describe.

2. Bowfell by the Climbers' Traverse

Follow The Band, or the path alongside Hell Gill, upwards until it levels off before the last rise up to Bowfell. Go a little way up the path after that, but veer off to the right to reach the shoulder, so that you can then peer over the great east-sloping face of Bowfell. The narrow path of the Climbers' Traverse should then be visible, winding an almost level way across the face, just below shattered crags. Straight ahead the path clings to the fellside aiming for the elegant, slim and soaring line of Bowfell Buttress, which rises conspicuously in Gothic splendour. I went that way one winter when the path was iced and there was hard, frozen snow all over the mountains, and my dog – a normally very sure-footed hound – slipped off the edge. I watched, completely powerless, as he skidded on the icy surface at a steady rate downhill, heading for Mickleden two thousand feet below. He didn't hit anything in his descent that I could see, but then to my great relief, something stopped him. After a few seconds he tottered to his feet, so I shouted and whistled encouragingly to him and he carefully started to walk back up the precise slope that he had just fallen down, but this time he very deliberately and delicately dug his claws into the frozen slope. With a few wags of his tail he was back on the path and none the worse for his escape.

As you get near to Bowfell Buttress the path goes under some gigantic and slightly overhanging crags (Cambridge Crags) where a little spring of water invariably gushes out to provide a welcome swig on a hot day. Bowfell Buttress has a classic climb. Originally graded 'Difficult' it has, over the years, been steadily upgraded so that, in damp conditions, it is probably now 'Severe'; this route is a splendid way to get up the buttress. If, however, rock-climbing is not your scene, you still have a couple of options.

The most attractive walkers' line to take is that which follows the right-hand edge of the Great Slab, a huge, tilted table of rock which forms the top of Flat Crags and separates them from Cambridge Crag above. To find this, immediately before crossing the scree gully to Bowfell Buttress, head leftwards up the rubble that has fallen from the crags above on to the Great Slab. There is a path of sorts and the angle is not severe, so that one soon arrives on the shoulder at its top; it is then but a few steps to join the main walkers' path from The Band. Bowfell summit is then in sight a couple of hundred yards away and in the distance are the Langdale Pikes.

Bowfell Buttress seen from the Climbers' Traverse.
Overleaf left: Great End and the Gables seen from Esk Pike.
Overleaf right: Great Knott and Crinkle Crags from Red Tarn.

The inferior way is to scrabble up the scree gully to the left of Bowfell Buttress itself. It is more immediately obvious, but it is a poor finish to the excellent Climbers' Traverse; it is hardly worth the trouble.

The actual summit of Bowfell is a fine viewpoint, particularly across to the Scafells and, if you are lucky enough to find the top reasonably free, there's room to sit and enjoy a sandwich. For the descent back to Langdale there are several attractive options.

You may choose to make a straightforward return down The Band – or more interestingly descend to Hell Gill and Oxendale. Another possibility is to reverse the Crinkle Crags Traverse. However, if you decide to head north-west, there is a well-cairned path over the boulder-fields to the Ore Gap (between Esk Pike and Bowfell) where an equally well-cairned path descends to Angle Tarn, a black pool under the cliffs of Hanging Knotts. The track then leads straightforwardly to Rossett Gill for the descent to Mickleden. However, possibly the most popular continuation of this walk is to go beyond the Ore Gap and toil up the rise to the sharp-jutting summit rocks of Esk Pike. There are fine views from there to Great End and Great Gable and an obvious descent to the high crossroads of Esk Hause. From that point you join the trade route back to Langdale via Angle Tarn and Rossett Gill.

If, however, time is running out and the longer alternatives are not feasible, you may still be in the mood for a little more adventurous descent than The Band or Oxendale. If so, then follow the cairned path towards the Ore Gap and Esk Pike, but keep to the edge of the crags heading north, until you can peep over the edge of what is Hanging Knotts to glimpse Angle Tarn far below your feet. You will notice the odd cairn which indicates a sketchy path swinging down the scree to the right of Hanging Knotts. This provides a rapid and safe way down to the hause between Rossett Gill and Angle Tarn. Alternatively, if you are not intimidated, ignore the cairns and look a little more closely. You will see that a few discriminating feet have unobtrusively started to mark a curving line of descent from one halting place to another – straight down Hanging Knotts. Sometimes you may feel that those feet can only have been those of a mountain-goat or a sheep, because the line is not at all clear from above. Later as you look up from below you will see that there is an obvious and logical line down grassy rakes and little ledges to the

right of the main gully that splits the shattered face. A bold approach is all that is needed to get you safely down almost to the level of Angle Tarn.

As you turn and scan the face you have just descended you will hardly fail to notice not just one, but a couple of rubble-filled gullies going back up to the summit ridge. Occasionally in winter they tempt the climber with hard-packed snow.

It is no great penance to have to ascend a hundred feet or so above Angle Tarn to get to the top of Rossett Gill for the descent to Langdale.

I once descended Rossett Gill in the dark, after a day on Scafell, but fortunately (for I have not always been so smart) I had remembered to pack my head torch. Also, I did recall and locate the zigzag line of descent down the true right-hand flank, which is a much better alternative to the straight up-and-down of the gill itself. This alternative gives a more amenable angle of descent, making it possible to go quite quickly, so long as you can see. However, I was on the last zigzag and got a great fright when I almost bumped into something which proved to be a man, literally on his hands and knees. He was very pleased to see me and it transpired that he could see very little without his glasses, which he had lost, nor had he a torch. His breeches were worn through, his knees were cut and bleeding, and he told me that he had been resigned to a night out, but had decided to get as low as possible first. I walked with him to the Dungeon Ghyll and left him telephoning his relatives to let them know he was safe.

3. Bowfell or Scafell Pike via Rossett Gill

This is not the most interesting way to go to Bowfell, but it is nowhere near as awful (the ascent of Rossett Gill in particular) as many of my friends and I myself used to consider it. The initial approach is a pleasant walk along the sheep-grazed sward of Mickleden from the Old Dungeon Ghyll to the bottom of Rossett Gill and then begins what used to be a steep and wearisome struggle, particularly near the top of the gill where the old watercourse was worn away to a hideous rubble by the boots of countless walkers. Happily, the gently graded pony track

on the left flank is very clearly marked and walkers are specifically urged not to go up the watercourse but to use the pony track instead. This is a much easier and better way of ascent. Frankly, only a masochist would prefer the older route.

What is perhaps not often realised is that there is yet another track even farther left. In descent this may just be spotted continuing along the line of the widest sweep that the pony-track makes. If you take this, it will enable you to cross the hillside just above the small but steep-sided gills that would otherwise impede your progress. You may then head gently downwards to reach a grassy ridge which eventually leads to the drumlin field farther down Mickleden, well beyond the bottom of Stake Pass.

This line appears to be longer than the well-marked pony track, but I have found it to be both pleasanter and quicker as a way down because it cuts off quite a big corner. Try it some time.

Once you've reached the top of Rossett Gill on your way to Bowfell, the most straightforward thing to do is to contour round Angle Tarn on the footpath that goes up to the Ore Gap. From there, head east across the stony wilderness towards Hanging Knotts and you will soon be on the summit of Bowfell.

If, on the other hand, Scafell Pike is your objective, once you reach Angle Tarn it is a simple matter to continue upwards beyond it to reach the four-sided stone windbreak on the col between Angle Tarn and Sprinkling Tarn. From here, a ninety-degree swing to the south-west, combined with a gentle climb over about three hundred yards, leads easily to Esk Hause. The main track now leads west to reach Calf Cove, where Victorian guides used to leave their ponies to drink where a little spring arises and graze what little grass there may be. Their riders then had to take to their own feet for the last mile to Scafell Pike, because the route crosses patches of large, sharp-edged rocks and boulders, which ponies could not negotiate at all without risk of broken legs. Even experienced fell-walkers need to take care here. A dip into the hause at the head of Little Narrowcove and a short climb then leads pleasantly to the summit of England's highest mountain.

Second Crinkle, Mickle Door and Third Crinkle, seen across Great Cove.

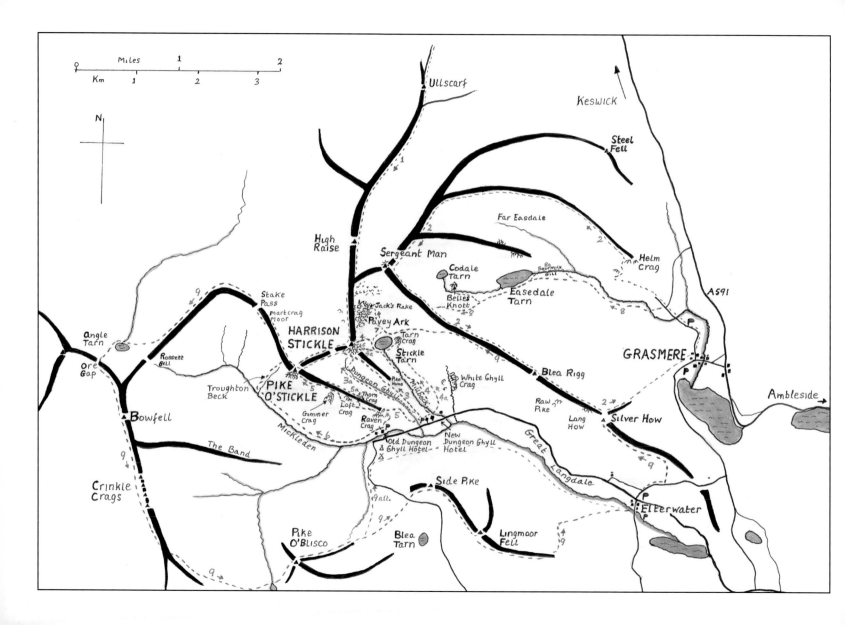

THE LANGDALE PIKES GROUP

	Approximate Time	Star Rating	Assessment of Difficulty
1. Keswick (or Dob Gill) to the Dungeon Ghyll Hotel, Great Langdale	5–8 hours	**	—
2. The Easedale Round	4–6 hours	*	—
3. Harrison Stickle via Dungeon Ghyll	4–5 hours	—	—
3a. Scrambles via Dungeon Ghyll and the south face of Harrison Stickle	add 1 1/2 hours	**	2
4. Harrison Stickle via Millbeck (Stickle Gill)	4–5 hours	*	—
4a. Alternative scrambles via Tarn Crag and east ridge of Harrison Stickle	add 1 1/2 hours	*	2
5. Pike o' Stickle from the New Dungeon Ghyll Hotel	4–5 hours	*	—
5a. Alternative scramble via Thorn Crag	add 1/2 hour	*	1–2
6. Pike o' Stickle from the Old Dungeon Ghyll via Stake Pass or Troughton Beck	4–5 hours	*	—
6a. Alternative scramble via Raven Crag and Loft Crag	add 3/4 hour	*	1–2
7. Langdale Pikes via Pavey Ark and Jack's Rake	4–5 hours	***	1
8. Sergeant Man and Langdale Pikes from Grasmere	5–6 hours	—	—
8a. Alternative scrambles via Sourmilk Gill and Belles Knott	1/2–1 hour	—	1–2
9. The Langdale Round	8–10 hours	***	—

THE LANGDALE PIKES GROUP

I don't know about reincarnation or the transmigration of souls but I sometimes imagine that if mine returns to this earth I would like it to be as a bird so that I could soar above the Lake District, wheeling and floating on the air over the fells, ghylls and crags. Every time I drive alongside Lake Windermere and see that classic and sometimes really wonderful view of the Langdale Pikes from near the Lowwood Hotel, I feel a lift of my spirits and a surge of hope for an adventurous day on the morrow. That view of the Pikes always stirs me and I know that I am not alone in this respect.

From the south, Langdale has the easiest access of all the great Lakeland valleys, but the valley and the peaks around its splendid skyline were, and to some extent still are, in danger of being destroyed by the visitors who come to enjoy them. Fortunately much work is being done to counteract the erosion and there are welcome signs that some footpaths are now beginning to recover. It is hardly a moment too soon, for around Langdale are some of the Lake District's finest views, a presentation of a variety of nature's most attractive forms in close juxtaposition and on a scale easily comprehended by the human mind and eye. No wonder that it is such a popular valley.

Consequently I am well aware that on the whole many people will know more about the Langdale Pikes than any other mountain group in the Lake District and I will therefore make the descriptions of very popular routes as brief as possible in order to concentrate on offering ideas about less well-known possibilities. Let's start with one of the longer walks, which, unusually for this book, is a traverse rather than a 'round'.

1. Keswick (or Dob Gill) to the Dungeon Ghyll Hotel, Great Langdale

The objective is to walk over as much as possible of the skyline ridge north to south. In one fell swoop you can cover all the main peaks of the Pikes group and have a terrific, if strenuous, day.

When I last did this walk it was from a starting point near Shoulthwaite Farm, at the Keswick end of the dual carriageway section of the A591 Ambleside-to-Keswick road and not strictly from Keswick, so that I could go up Shoulthwaite Gill and have a closer look at the notorious Iron Crag. Apparently the Gill is on a geological faultline and Iron Crag has a reputation for looseness which deters all but intrepid rock-climbers.

It looked to me as if there was at least one good, solid buttress on the crag though whether or not the crag itself was safely attached to the fellside I am not qualified to say. Anyway, there is a reasonable path as far as the crag by courtesy of the Forestry Commission. Thereafter you must take to the bracken and the lumps and bumps of tussocky grass that make for tough going until you reach High Seat at a height of 1,996 feet. From there it's along the watershed above Watendlath in Borrowdale, over Middle Crag, Shivery Knott and Long Moss, to skirt another Blea Tarn, having picked up the Wythburn-to-Watendlath footpath for part of the way. The word 'watershed' is particularly inappropriate in this case, because an enormous amount of it seems to be retained, rather than shed, in the bogs and peaty groughs which one must walk to reach Ullscarf.

(For a shorter and possibly more convenient walk you could make use of the good Forestry Commission car park at Dob Gill on the west side of

Thirlmere. A footpath from there leads through the conifers past Harrop Tarn to gain the main ridge just about a mile north of Ullscarf.)

About a mile after Ullscarf, on a wide and obvious grassy col, you will cross the main path between Far Easedale and Borrowdale. Thereafter you also are on a good path and may head up the peaty and boggy slope to High White Stones and High Raise at 2,500 feet, which are the highest points on a broad and stony dome. While you are there don't miss the opportunity to 'bag' Sergeant Man. Its little pimple of a summit is only half a mile away across the plateau and there are splendid views ahead to Pavey Ark and Harrison Stickle.

Shortly after leaving Sergeant Man you should get your first sight of Stickle Tarn nestling in the hollow below the great cirque of crags formed by Pavey Ark and Harrison Stickle. The path traverses a maze of rocky humps and lies well back from the steepest crags, so it isn't until you have scrambled up to the square rocky platform of Harrison Stickle's summit that you will really see much of the view back to the dramatic cliff of Pavey Ark. Down to the south-east lies the long, green Langdale valley, a patchwork of fields and stone walls, white cottages and farm buildings, varied by the sparkle of light glinting on becks and tarns all the way down to Elterwater and beyond. It is the reverse of the classic view from Lowwood.

If you get wet feet on the stretch to Ullscarf, or are looking for any other acceptable excuse for yourself or your companions to call it a day, this is the opportunity. If, however, you can summon up enough energy to bag Pike o' Stickle, do so, then head off briskly west down a stony and well-battered slope to cross the depression that leads up to the rocky cone of Pike o' Stickle. It will take only a quarter of an hour or so and you'll again have that superb view down Langdale, but with the drama heightened considerably, because this time your gaze will sweep over the great south-east face of Gimmer Crag with its splendid rock-climbing, while across the valley floor, beyond Side Pike, Blea Tarn shines like a pearl.

There are, as you will either know or realise, three or four ways to descend into Mickleden from the Pikes. I think that from Pike o' Stickle it is possibly best to get back to the path in the depression between the Pikes where Dungeon Ghyll begins and take the path that follows the left-hand side of the beck. As soon as the stream tumbles away down the ravine, which is the upper part of Dungeon Ghyll, the path strikes across the flanks of Harrison Stickle, above the waters on the left-hand side.

It is sometimes a place where the wind may funnel down with great ferocity. I recall one winter's day when, with a friend, we had mistakenly thought that we might

The Langdale Pikes seen from The Band.

enjoy a good day's skiing up there, but our efforts were in vain for there was not enough good snow, just a lot of ice and sharp rocks. To descend the path that day we had to shuffle and slither down on our backsides – not the correct thing to do when carrying skis and sticks as well. My reward was that I secured a really marvellous photograph down Rossett Gill, with the Pikes emerging briefly from mist.

Normally there is a fast descent to a proud little rock castle – a sort of mini-Harrison Stickle called Pike Howe – which is well worth a visit. From that point there is a good back view of the upper waterfall of Dungeon Ghyll and you can take a last look down Langdale before the stony descent to the Stickle Barn or the car park beside the New Dungeon Ghyll Hotel.

2. The Easedale Round, incorporating Helm Crag, Sergeant Man, Blea Rigg and Raw Pike

As one ascends the Dunmail Raise road from Grasmere towards Keswick the eye of fancy sees 'the Lion and the Lamb', an intriguing rock formation on the skyline to the left. Situated on Helm Crag these rocks are at the first high point on this most enjoyable round. Don't try to park up the Easedale road out of Grasmere; the car park that used to be situated just south of Goody Bridge has been turned into a 'low-cost' housing development, so you'll have a short extra walk from the village.

At the end of the metalled road near Easedale House the correct path is signposted for Far Easedale (the old packhorse route over to Borrowdale) and also for Helm Crag. The old path to Helm Crag went more or less straight up the steep fellside and was very badly eroded but now there is a well-engineered route that skirts the right edge of Helm Crag proper. In graded curves it then goes round on to the shoulder of the fell before there is a last pull up to the summit rocks where the 'Lion' and the 'Lamb' will be in hiding. The ridge, which is the retaining wall of Far Easedale, stretches away before you, with rocky knobbles and peaty passages but with mostly easy walking on a good path. As you pace it there are good views to Fairfield on one side while across the dale in the other direction, south-west, you will be able to pick out Deer Bield Crag. The great buttress leaning against the crag has slipped noticeably since the early editions of this book and there is clearly a risk of more movement in the future. Before then, in the 1980s, I recall having a fright when I climbed Deer Bield Chimney, as I felt certain that the rocks were moving as I clung to them, so I will not be tempting fate again myself.

Eventually you reach the hause to which the path rises from Far Easedale. Here, there is a curiosity: a cast-iron stile standing all alone with virtually no other sign of a fence. It has obviously not stopped a sheep for many a year and now it is people who climb over it for a laugh. Perhaps it helps sheep with their sleepless nights?

If you wheel right (north-west) at this point and descend to the bog below you will emerge from the morass at the Greenup Ghyll–High Raise ridge, but it is better to go straight across the col at right-angles to the line of Far Easedale. A faint path heads up the left bank of the beck, leaving it as height is gained, but still going south-west along the line of an old fence to reach the plateau at Codale Head. The rocky little summit of Sergeant Man is then just a few hummocks farther away, and you can scramble up to its summit secure in the knowledge that from then on it is downhill all the way. The descent is to the south-east along the broad ridge between Codale Tarn and Stickle Tarn to the knobbles of Blea Rigg, then Swinescar Hause, (where a path crosses the ridge between Great Langdale and Easedale). Your path skirts the sites of two now virtually overgrown tarns, under the rocky top of Lang How, which were colonised for years by black-headed gulls. Now the water has virtually disappeared under reeds and the gulls do not bother coming any more. From here the path quickly swings north-east to the top of the Wray Gill, above Grasmere. Unless you prefer a steep, stony, brackeny and slithery descent down this, which I do not recommend, keep to the north side of the gill and follow the clear path to the left (north-east) towards Easedale through attractive clumps of ancient juniper and a bouldery walled lane. You will soon reach reach the Easedale road out of Grasmere and the end of a most satisfying tramp.

Two ways up Harrison Stickle, with optional scrambles

All the way up Langdale, and particularly from beyond Chapel Stile, it is the splendid view of the Pikes and the great cliff of Pavey Ark which catch the eye. After Helvellyn the ascent of the Pikes must be among the most popular walks in the Lake District. I will therefore describe two routes for the first-time visitor, but would like also to mention alternative ways that may appeal to the jaded palates of those who think they've done it all and need tempting with something a little different.

Both of the main paths for Harrison Stickle start from the large car parks near the New Dungeon Ghyll Hotel. One path goes via Dungeon Ghyll (the

On the Easedale Round: a winter view to Fairfield and St Sunday Crag.

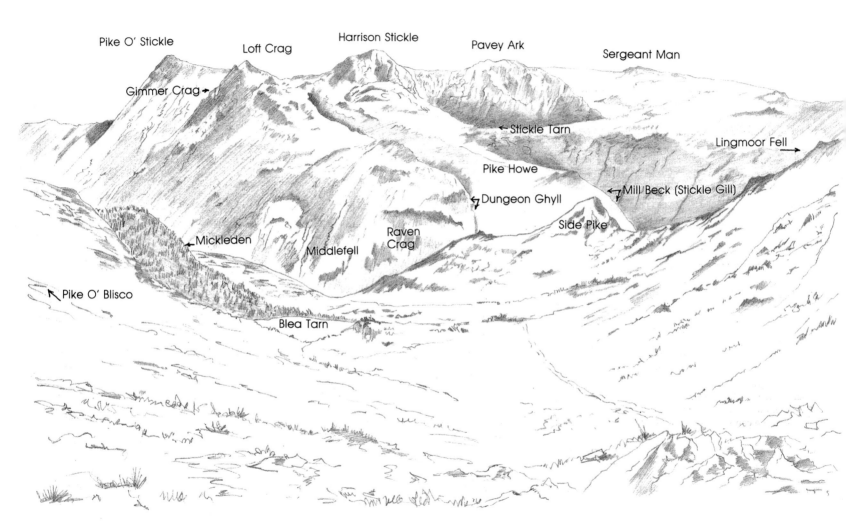

Pike O' Stickle

Loft Crag

Harrison Stickle

Pavey Ark

Sergeant Man

Gimmer Crag →

← Stickle Tarn

Lingmoor Fell →

Pike Howe

← Mill Beck (Stickle Gill)

↙ Dungeon Ghyll

Side Pike

← Mickleden

Raven Crag

Middlefell

← Pike O' Blisco

Blea Tarn

ravine not the bar!) while the second one goes up to Stickle Tarn via Millbeck (Stickle Gill). I'll start with the former:

3. Harrison Stickle via Dungeon Ghyll

Immediately on leaving the car parks and beyond the buildings, bear left away from the obvious path coming down Millbeck (also called Stickle Gill) and follow the other path leftwards through a gate in the wall on the end of the ridge to a stile, which leads to the foaming beck rushing down Dungeon Ghyll. If the beck is crossed using big stones at this point you will get on to what is probably the best footpath for Gimmer Crag and Pike o' Stickle, which leads up the left-bounding ridge of Dungeon Ghyll. This time do not cross the beck but keep to the right up a partly stepped path, continuing up to the rocky point of Pike Howe. The path then follows a rising line well above the right bank of the ghyll towards its head. It leads to a more level, but more exposed, traverse which cuts across the defile at the head of the ghyll. (Along here you are below the steep rocks of Harrison Stickle's south-east flank.) After leaving the head of the ghyll bear round to the right (north-east) and so go up to the summit by using either of two obvious rocky tracks.

3a. Scrambles via Dungeon Ghyll and the south face of Harrison Stickle

If taken throughout this is a splendidly varied way to the summit of Harrison Stickle, because it links two scrambles together.

Instead of going up the path – as in the previous walk – high above the right bank of the ravine of Dungeon Ghyll, take instead a narrow path up the ravine itself, which starts just on the right of the stream. (In summer bracken tends to obscure this somewhat.) After a diversion to view the gloomy depths of the 'dungeon' this path leads to a point above the main waterfall. Just before the trees end there are a couple of interesting scrambly passages, but then, after a level section, the ravine begins to bend to the right and is closed by an amphitheatre with a long waterslide. Scramble up the right-hand side then enter a zone of large boulders through which the stream splashes. There is a footpath through them, but some good scrambling can be had in the stream bed itself, particularly near an archway formed by two huge boulders. The ravine levels out again as it bends back to the left and it is easy walking into the upper amphitheatre with its impressive cascade. There appears to be no exit, but there is a way, which becomes evident as you get right up to the waterfall itself, up a little rib of rock leading to a gully on the left side. This leads nicely upwards out of the amphitheatre to a steep finish on the fellside above the falls.

The next part of our way should be clearly visible, ahead and on the other side of the stream, so cross this easily, toil up a grassy slope beyond and join the main path.

At the point where this ascending path up the right flank of Dungeon Ghyll passes most closely to steep rocks above it (the rocks of Harrison Stickle) there is a rather steep and intimidating buttress whose lowest rocks are only a few feet above the track. Do not be put off by this. I used to do this scramble with both my two small dogs. Now I do it just with one, Freddie the Second, the survivor. Just go round the steep rocks on their right-hand side and scramble up a grassy and slightly overhung rake to reach a wide and grassy sloping shelf. Trend rightwards then, towards the apparent edge of the buttress, and you will find sharp little ledges giving splendid incut holds. These lead upwards and over to a series of grassy ledges interspersed with little rock walls. There is no one obvious way and you can go up the grassy ledges if you want to, but it is more fun to link together little rocky passages which make it possible to scramble all the way to the summit platform. Even my dog enjoys it – and what a marvellous alternative for the experienced scrambler!

4. Harrison Stickle via Millbeck (Stickle Gill)

For the second main footpath to Harrison Stickle, that via Millbeck and Stickle Tarn, the chances are high that a few hundred others will have preceded you already today, but the path has been rescued from the worst effects of boots and erosion and is nowhere near as awful as it used to be. The main path, which starts on the left bank of Millbeck, crosses over to the right at a footbridge above the trees, re-crosses on large boulders high up the gill and emerges at the outflow of Stickle Tarn, with its splendid view across to the cliffs of Pavey Ark. For Harrison Stickle one then swings left around the edge of the tarn and then ascends an obvious path which skirts steeply under the rocky east ridge of the peak and then curves back round to the summit rocks. Very straightforward; not very exciting.

4a. Alternative scrambles via Tarn Crag and the east ridge of Harrison Stickle

Here are a couple of more adventurous alternatives. Firstly, instead of leaving the car park and heading up the Millbeck path, follow instead the signs for White

Gill crag alongside the walled-in stream bed. When the signs point rightwards through a gate for White Gill ignore them and instead go straight ahead. The path will lead nicely to a steeper path up the fellside and so to the lowest rocks of Tarn Crag, which is on the right at the head of Millbeck. (The tourist path will now be below, on the left.)

The main features of this crag are two ribs of rock and a central bay with trees between them. Just to the right of the right-hand rib, which is fairly steep and much more of a rock-climb, there is a slighter rib of rock which is more broken up and yields a very pleasant scramble for a couple of hundred feet or so right to the summit of Tarn Crag. This is an even better viewpoint for the cliffs of Pavey Ark and it also gives a better view of my suggested alternative scrambling way to the summit of Harrison Stickle. This is to tackle the East Ridge itself instead of the rather wearisome footpath below it. This ridge really consists of three rock tiers linked by terraces which enable you to avoid the rather smooth and difficult lower rocks.

From Stickle Tarn go up the worn path towards Harrison Stickle and towards the rocks of the first steep barrier. Instead of evading this on the right, as the path does, slant leftwards instead and evade it that way. Now a wide grassy terrace leads back right below a second rock tier. Very experienced scramblers may climb directly on good holds up the rocks of this second tier, but it is exposed and most people (including me) keep going right on ledges until you may zigzag back left and upwards, avoiding the steep rock, to reach an easier angled rock ridge.

The rock ridge attained gives very pleasant scrambling on rock covered in rugosities and wrinkles and leads to another grassy terrace below a steep upper wall. A sheep track on the left gives the easiest upward progress but rocky ledges slanting leftwards across the wall from the top of the terrace give a more sporting way of climbing higher. All that remains is an easy walk to the summit rocks but the views over Stickle Tarn and the cliffs of Pavey Ark are very dramatic. It is an excellent and little-used way to the heights. (Incidentally, this same east ridge of Harrison Stickle gives a very pleasant and rapid descent from the summit to Stickle Tarn.)

Pike o' Stickle: two footpaths and some alternative scrambles

The rocky cone of Pike o' Stickle is an even better viewpoint than Harrison Stickle and to climb it is usually a visually rewarding experience, but again I would like to offer some alternative ways to get there.

5. Pike o' Stickle from the New Dungeon Ghyll Hotel

Starting from the car parks near the New Hotel the best footpath is that which goes up the left bank of the stream of the Dungeon Ghyll (bear left instead of going straight up Millbeck on leaving the car park), but if you've never seen them don't fail to have a look at the lower falls of Dungeon Ghyll. At the start the path up the left bank stays close to the edge of the ghyll, then, just before it leaves it, and almost hidden in some trees, a magnificent wedged boulder bridges the chasm and is a fine viewpoint for the sixty-foot waterfall that leaps into the gloomy recesses below. It is quite feasible to cross the bridge, but nervous souls will wisely avoid it.

The path then climbs the hillside, leaving the edge of the ghyll, and you will have to puff upwards past Thorn Crag on the right. It is then up and around the back of Loft Crag, which extends in a broken sweep to enfold the eastern end of the splendid rock playground of Gimmer Crag. The crest of the ridge is reached and only a few hundred yards away are the wonderful views from the summit, particularly down Langdale overlooking the south-west face of Gimmer.

5a. Alternative scramble via Thorn Crag

As an alternative with a bit more spice of adventure in it, you can scramble up Thorn Crag, which has perfect rough rock. To find this scramble, having toiled up the path on the left edge of Dungeon Ghyll and then reached the grassy plateau beyond, watch carefully for the ruined stone walls of a small sheepfold and make for the broken rocky ridge near and above it. This gives the general line of the route, though as usual you need to pick out the most continuous rock for best enjoyment in the early stages. There is a broad terrace below the rocks of the upper buttress, and the best way is to climb up the rocks from its right-hand edge and then by slabs, walls and ribs in fine, open situations right to the top. Pike o' Stickle is now close at hand, just beyond the top of Loft Crag, and easily reached.

6. Pike o' Stickle from the Old Dungeon Ghyll via Stake Pass or Troughton Beck

The road doesn't go any farther up Mickleden itself than the Old Dungeon Ghyll Hotel. Thereafter the valley wall on the northern side is steeper and access to the summit ridge is defended by the buttresses of Raven Crag and steep screes. It is true that there is a long slanting footpath which ascends the fellside from near the Old Dungeon Ghyll to the base of Gimmer Crag, which may be

picked out without much difficulty, but it is much more suitable as a means of descent for climbers (who rarely go up that way) than as an ascent route for walkers. Alternatively you may walk up Mickleden, firstly on a stony track alongside the wall that runs halfway along the valley floor and then over the close-cropped grass towards the drumlins at the bottom of Rossett Gill. Instead of tackling the gill, ascend rightwards up the long slopes of the Stake Pass. This is a pleasant enough way, though it is more a toil than a pleasure tramping up Martcrag Moor and it seems to take for ever to get to Pike o' Stickle.

However, there is a less-used and more direct way on a grassy path up the left bank of Troughton Beck. This is the stream that begins at about 1,700 feet on the edge of Martcrag Moor, halfway between Pike o' Stickle and the Stake Pass. Although the path is not easily seen from below, the stream line is clear enough and it shouldn't be too difficult to choose a line upwards that will enable you to join it and so go on to Pike o' Stickle. This approach does have the merit of enabling a circular tour to be made of all the main peaks without having to double back on your tracks.

6a. Alternative scramble via on Raven Crag and Loft Crag

For a more exciting scrambling way, however, you must accept the challenge of the craggy fellside immediately behind the O.D.G. as a way to higher places. Walkers with plenty of rock-climbing experience will omit the first pitch and then climb the remainder of Middlefell Buttress, which is narrower and next to the main buttress of Raven Crag; it has for many years been the rock-climber's staircase to Gimmer Crag. However, this is definitely more of a rock-climb than a scramble. An easier alternative is to walk to the right, from the bottom of Middlefell Buttress below the steeper buttress of Raven Crag, and go up the gully on its right-hand side. As the gully steepens it is necessary to go leftwards on a path up ledges until one arrives amongst large blocks of rock. A little descent, then a scramble up these, using a large spiky block to gain some height lands you immediately on easier ground at the top of the buttress. It is only about ten feet of steep scrambling amongst the blocks. A straightforward ascent by ledges, little walls and grassy terraces up the fellside leads to the path heading for the Pikes from the New Dungeon Ghyll Hotel. As a pleasant and interesting way of gaining necessary height it could hardly be bettered.

If you then go along the path towards the Pikes for a little way you will spot the almost level track that is the climbers' approach to Gimmer Crag. This leads to an enjoyable scramble on the three-stepped buttress of Loft Crag. This should be easily spotted since it is well to the right of the very steep rock wall bounded by the South East Gully which identifies Gimmer Crag. On Loft Crag the first 'step' is very easy, the second is steeper but the difficult rock may be avoided by following the slanting gangway on its right edge. Thereafter the way is obvious with a pleasant sense of exposure near the top. Pike o' Stickle is then only a short distance away.

7. Langdale Pikes via Pavey Ark and Jack's Rake

The great cliff of Pavey Ark is a marvellous playground (or sometimes battleground!) for rock-climbers, and although it appears very vegetated when viewed from a distance, that impression is soon dispelled once one sets foot on it. From an active fell-walker's point of view, however, it is particularly special, because of the existence of the superb slanting line of Jack's Rake which cuts right across the crag from bottom right to top left, thus making it by far the most attractive way of reaching the top. The line is easily seen from the opposite side of Stickle Tarn. To ascend Pavey Ark by Jack's Rake must surely be the most popular scramble in Lakeland and this exciting outing must be on every fell-walker's list.

The bottom of Pavey Ark may be reached by the approach up Millbeck (Stickle Gill), and if you wish to avoid Jack's Rake you can go round Stickle Tarn well away from the cliffs to find a well-worn path up loose stones that leads to the top. Avoid the struggle up an even more hideous way called Scree Gully, which goes directly up the stone-shoot on the right of and below the almost vertical east-face rocks. It has deteriorated very noticeably in the last twenty years, with awkward, loose rocks to negotiate low down and even more awkward ones higher up. Leave it to the rock-climbers.

No, there is no doubt about it; Jack's Rake is definitely the way to the top of Pavey Ark. Although it traverses the whole of this great cliff there is little sense of exposure, for the path – and a lot of the way there is a path – goes up a sort of groove which gives a good sense of security. You only emerge from the groove when you are quite high up the cliff, by which time you have got used to being up there anyway. Right at the end of the rising traverse there are a couple of rock steps to negotiate, but even these can be avoided by following a level track round to the

Far left: Jack's Rake: looking back from half way up.
Left: On Jack's Rake, near the top.

left, into an easy grassy gully which leads to the top of the cliff. From Pavey there is a footpath over rough and rocky ground towards Harrison Stickle.

Whenever I go up Jack's Rake nowadays I recall a hair-raising experience with a peregrine falcon. I was rock-climbing on a route called Stickle Grooves, which starts at the bottom of Jack's Rake, and I was on a steep slab split by a thin crack. I had just reached the top of the slab and was about to pull over on to a large ledge when there was a sudden screech and a rush of wings and I nearly fell off backwards with the shock. Unwittingly I had found the peregrine's nest, and the female bird had been sitting on a clutch of eggs. Incidentally, using the Rake as a descent is more problematical than as an ascent because of the difficulty in finding the right starting place, so my advice would be: if you haven't been up it, don't attempt to go down it, until you know what to expect. (Climber-walkers who know the crag will enjoy a descent from the middle of Jack's Rake down the line of Crescent Climb. I only realised this possibility myself in the recent past.)

8. Sergeant Man and the Langdale Pikes from Grasmere

Apart from climbing Sergeant Man as part of the Easedale round already mentioned there is a well-signed and very popular path heading towards Sergeant Man which goes up Easedale itself. From Grasmere walk up Easedale Road (opposite Sam Read's bookshop) until signs for Easedale Tarn lead over a bridge across the stream. By going along the left bank through sheep pastures it leads to a rocky path up Sourmilk Gill, emerging at Easedale Tarn. The path then runs a little way back from the left bank of the tarn and climbs some rock slabs up a steeper section to the level of the much smaller Codale Tarn. A final pull up the fellside on a fair path and you are on the ridge above Blea Rigg. Sergeant Man is half a mile away and the Pikes are a little farther, of course.

8a. Alternative scrambles via Sourmilk Gill and Belles Knott

As an entertaining alternative, by which I mean, of course, a scrambling variation, you may choose to clamber up the rocks in the stream bed of Sourmilk Gill until it reaches the level of Easedale Tarn.

Beyond the tarn the path is fairly level for a time, but as it starts to climb it is worth moving on to the rocks in the stream bed (Easedale Gill) as the beck runs over a series of cascades towards a rocky knoll marked on the map as Belles Knott, and behind which lies Codale Tarn. While leaving the rocks of the gill you can head up the slope and make an entertaining scramble on excellent rock right up the skyline edge of Belles Knott. For a little while it feels as though you might be on a real mountain – until all too soon you reach its level and grassy top.

9. The Langdale Round

This must, of course, rate as one of the longest and best day's walking in the district. Several variations are possible: for instance, starting up Dungeon Ghyll and going directly to the Pikes. Of course this reduces the time required by about two hours but sadly it also omits the pleasant section above Elterwater from Silver How to Harrison Stickle.

My own choice of route for this great round is in an anti-clockwise direction. Start at Elterwater village and go northwards to the end of the ridge at the top of Red Bank. Then go north-west to Silver How, Raw Pike, Blea Rigg and descend to Stickle Tarn. From there it is up the always enjoyable scramble of Jack's Rake across the face of the great cliff of Pavey Ark and so on to Harrison Stickle. The next summit is, of course, Pike o' Stickle, followed by the long descent over Martcrag Moor to the head of the Stake Pass. It is well known that the slopes just below the summit of Pike o' Stickle were one of Stone Age Man's tool-making sites and I have found partly worked axe-heads on the moor to the north of the Pike. However, I have been even more surprised to find plenty of trout in the little feeder streams of the Stake Beck at around two thousand feet. I wonder how on earth they got there.

This descent of Martcrag Moor to the top of the Stake Pass can be very wet and it is usually so on the next section to Angle Tarn. It is then a tough climb up to the Ore Gap and then Bowfell summit before the Crinkles. This is a wearisome trudge towards the end of a long day before ascending to Pike o'Blisco. After the descent of Pike o' Blisco you should strictly include Side Pike and Lingmoor Fell before descending to Elterwater. For some reason or other – probably too tired! – I have never done that myself but have preferred to nurse my weary feet down Great Langdale's footpaths to Elterwater to complete the circuit. It is a challenging but unforgettable day.

Pavey ark seen from Harrison Stickle.

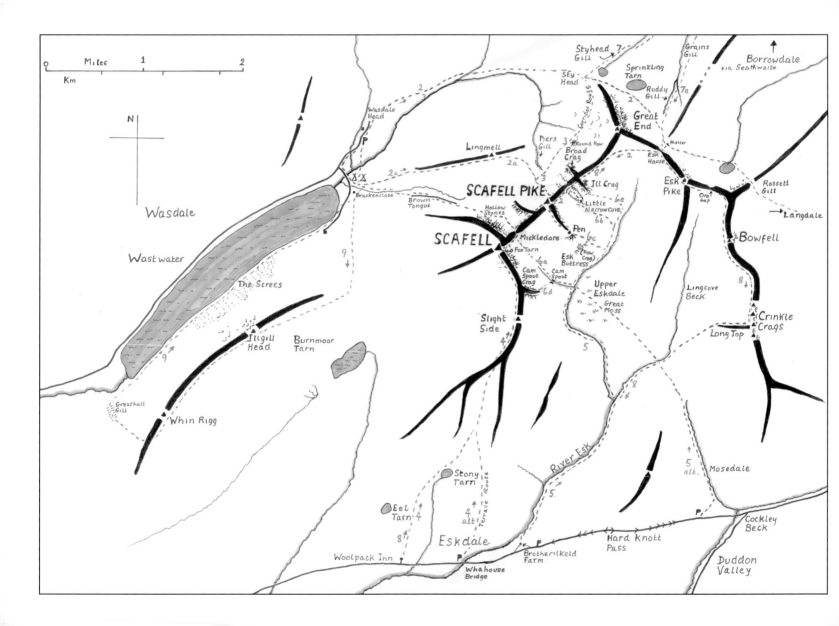

THE SCAFELL GROUP

	Approximate Time	Star Rating	Assessment of Difficulty
SCAFELL PIKE TO SCAFELL			
1a. Via Foxes Tarn	3/4–1 hour	*	—
1b. Via Broad Stand	1/2–3/4 hour	*	3 (but only for 20 feet)
1c. Via Lord's Rake and the west wall traverse of Deep Ghyll	3/4–1 hour	***	1–2
1d. Via the continuation of Lord's Rake	3/4–1 hour	*	1
ROUTES FROM WASDALE			
2. Scafell Pike and/or Scafell from Wasdale via Styhead and Esk Hause	5–7 hours	**	—
2a. Reverse of the previous route via Lingmell Spur	5–7 hours	**	—
3. Scafell Pike or Scafell via the Corridor Route	5–7 hours	***	—
3a. Alternative scrambles on Round How and Broad Crag	add 1 hour	*	2
ROUTES FROM ESKDALE			
4. Scafell via Stony Tarn and Slight Side	6–8 hours	*	—
5. Approaches to Upper Eskdale via the Esk or from Cockley Beck	1–2 hours	—	—
6. Footpaths to the Scafells from Upper Eskdale:			
6a. Via Cam Spout to Mickledore	1 hour	*	—
6b. Via Little Narrowcove	1 hour	—	—
6c. Scramble to Scafell Pike via Pen	1–2 hours	***	3
6d. Scramble to Scafell via Edge of Cam Spout Crag	1 hour	*	1
6e. Scramble to Scafell Pike via Ill Crag	1–2 hours	***	1–3
ROUTES FROM BORROWDALE			
7. Scafell Pike or Scafell via Styhead Gill	5–7 hours	***	—
7a. The Scafells via Grains Gill with optional scramble en route in Ruddy Gill	add 1/2 hour	***	1–2
8. The Eskdale Round	7–10 hours	***	3 (for Broad Stand)
9. The Wasdale Screes Traverse	3–4 hours	*	—

THE SCAFELL GROUP

This group of fells contains England's highest mountain, Scafell Pike, but this is only the highest point on a great massif of high land which has fine cliffs and superb mountain scenery of impressive grandeur – splendid without being overpowering.

There are a number of well-known and well-trodden paths to review, but there is also a great deal of virtually untrodden ground and it is possible to reach most of the tops by slightly more devious, but often much more interesting, routes than the normal tourist paths. Especially for the fell-walker who already has some experience of these hills, these other ways can give added enjoyment and present totally new aspects of what before seemed familiar. I hope that my descriptions of them will provide some new inspiration.

Wasdale Head was the cradle of the sport of rock-climbing in Britain and it is over a century since W. P. Haskett-Smith made his solo ascent of Napes Needle on Great Gable and so provided an 'official' beginning. Fell-walking and scrambling are, of course, part of the same movement but it is in some ways a little strange that Wasdale Head should have assumed such significance, for it is not easy to get there from the major population areas farther south. Furthermore the peaks at the northern end of Wastwater present the first barrier to the moisture-laden clouds scudding across the Atlantic and consequently rainfall is higher there than farther east. Nevertheless, even excluding Scafell Pike, this area probably contains the greatest concentration of really shapely peaks in the Lake District. These mountains form a compact mass lying north-east to south-west and the north-eastern edge of it is a very steep escarpment – Great End – which continues at around the 3,000-foot level (900 metres) over Ill Crag and Broad Crag to Scafell Pike. It then descends a little to the narrow ridge of Mickledore before rising in the abrupt walls of the East and North Buttresses of Scafell, which have some of the region's finest rock-climbing. Beyond the summit of Scafell the ridge swings south, drops a little to Slight Side (which is just a distinct point on the ridge) and then declines gently towards Brotherilkeld in Eskdale. Crossing from Scafell Pike to Scafell, however, does present quite a problem to the fell-walker because the two peaks are very different in character. Since this key passage appears in many of the walks and scrambles in this chapter it would seem a good idea to deal first of all with the different options available for linking Scafell Pike and Scafell. There have been important changes to note.

Scafell Pike to Scafell

1a. Via Foxes Tarn

More people cross Mickledore from Scafell Pike to Scafell than in the reverse direction and the route via Foxes Tarn is probably the longest but also the safest. It involves descending below the cliffs of the East Buttress (on the left from Mickledore) and then following a narrow path underneath the buttress so as to outflank it. Climb up a wide square-cut gully with a stream running down it, then up an easier section to reach the tiny Foxes Tarn sheltering under the shattered crags. The eroded scree path was replaced by a stone staircase, although this is now also disintegrating, emerging from the depths near the summit. For ascent or descent this route is probably also the safest under bad weather conditions or if there is poor visibility.

1b. Via Broad Stand

This is the most direct way to the top of Scafell from Mickledore and it finds a way up the sloping rock ledges at the west end of the ridge. It has one 'bad step' on it which is a potential disaster-point, particularly if wet and it can occasionally present an insuperable problem even to experienced rock-climbers.

I have been to the assistance of walking parties in difficulty on at least four occasions in the past thirty years, needing a rope on three of them, so it is wise not to attempt this route unless you have rock-climbing experience or are with people who have. It is not that it is 'desperate'. In dry conditions there is very little problem for a reasonably agile person and so long as the initial approach from Mickledore is by squeezing through the vertical cleft – a 'fat man's agony' – on the left of the ridge, the way thereafter is well-marked. The hardest bit is the slightly overhanging corner about eight feet high and only twenty-five feet or so above the level of Mickledore, but it is in an exposed position. There is strong evidence that Samuel Taylor Coleridge made the first descent of this route in 1803. After the corner it is plain scrambling to the top of the crag, with splendid views across Scafell Pinnacle and down Deep Ghyll towards Great Gable and the Pillar Group. The summit of Scafell is not the nearest high point to catch your eye above the crags of Deep Ghyll, for it is a couple of hundred yards away and many are the rock-climbers who have climbed on the crags and never visited it. The Dedicated Fell-walker goes there automatically, of course.

Mickledore Ridge, Broad Stand and Scafell.

1c. Via Lord's Rake and the west wall traverse of Deep Ghyll

Lord's Rake passes under the magnificent and sometimes intimidating cliffs of the north face, giving a fell-walker a taste of the grandeur of this tremendous rock scenery. Both this route and the next, the Continuation of Lord's Rake, used to be standard ways. No more. A footpath skirts directly below the foot of the crags, leading directly into Lord's Rake, a rock-walled ravine leading fairly steeply upwards. It used to have plenty of scree in it, but nowadays there is much more earth and it feels much more precarious underfoot. Much worse, a large rock has fallen and lies wedged at the top of this first rise, on a little col. Over the years Lord's Rake has seen its share of accidents, but this is different. I have been up to it and past it to make my own assessment of the risk. It seems well jammed at present, but the place above – from which it became detached – must now be unstable and it is quite possible that more rocks will fall from above, especially during or after bad weather. This is why there are notices on the approach footpaths warning of the risks. If you do walk along the footpath towards the Rake you may well be able to distinguish the unique Flake Crack on Central Buttress, rated for some years as the hardest climb in Britain. However, that too has changed: the chockstone wedged beside the Great Flake fell out (after being used as the anchor point for rope or tape slings for about a century) and caused the death of the unfortunate climber resting below. The 'eternal hills' are always changing.

Immediately afterwards you will pass below Moss Ghyll, with more echoes from the golden age of mountaineering. This is a route I will always remember because I climbed it with one of our dogs in my rucksack. He complained a bit when I bumped his head as I was leading the Collie Step, but it did not do him any lasting harm and he certainly preferred to go up the climb to being left behind.

If, and I emphasise the 'if', you do go up Lord's Rake, just before you reach the top of the first rise, look out for the narrow path of the West Wall Traverse which rises upwards and sharply leftwards. It rapidly improves and leads on to rocky ledges which bypass the steep lower reaches of Deep Ghyll. However, what used to be a simple scramble up scree is now a much nastier proposition. The scree has gone; packed red earth at a very steep angle with virtually no soundly anchored rocks is what remains and you have to treat it as if it were snow. Considering the risks involved in getting to the point where you step on to the West Wall Traverse and then those involved in climbing up the rest of Deep Ghyll, it is not an attractive proposition.

1d. Via the Continuation of Lord's Rake

Continuing in the line of Lord's Rake, which would involve passing the jammed rock, the path descends slightly then curves up to a second little col before a scramble up broken ground leads to the shoulder and it is then just a short pull up to the summit of Scafell. This used to be a very good alternative route in either ascent or descent. As stated above, I have been up Lord's Rake to the jammed boulder and I have also been past it on a descent from the summit of Scafell. If you do the same, you take the risk. I can not recommend either of these routes again until the ground above stabilises.

Descending from Scafell to Mickledore means reversing the previous routes, of course. The safest for a fell-walker is the Foxes Tarn route. The quickest way down is Broad Stand, so long as you know what you are doing. The Deep Ghyll route and the Continuation of Lord's Rake (but in descent) are not justifiable at time of writing. On the other hand, if you simply aim to return to Wasdale, the most convenient way from the summit is to head west away from the edge of the cliffs and then down the grassy slopes to the Burnmoor Tarn–Wasdale track.

Having covered the crucial link between Scafell Pike and Scafell we can now have a look at the classic routes to either summit, firstly from Wasdale Head.

ROUTES FROM WASDALE

2. Scafell Pike and/or Scafell via Styhead and Esk Hause

This is a splendid day on the fells and well worth the effort. Beyond the Wastwater Head Inn the path leads up through the well-cropped grass of the intake fields. If you are really lucky you might still see the famous fell-runner Joss Naylor, running up the fell chasing sheep – while his dog whistles! Then it is north-east along the line of the Lingmell Beck, with the scree slopes of Great Gable on the left.

The path is broad and obvious, and yet – I can hardly believe it myself now – I once lost it completely. I had descended by mistake into Wasdale rather than Borrowdale because of thick mist and consequently had to try to walk back to Borrowdale over Styhead, up this very track. I had a pint at the pub – but only one! – and then tramped steadily uphill in the mist and darkness along the track, until I realised that somehow I was no longer on it. Even with a good torch it remained 'lost' for nearly an hour and was only

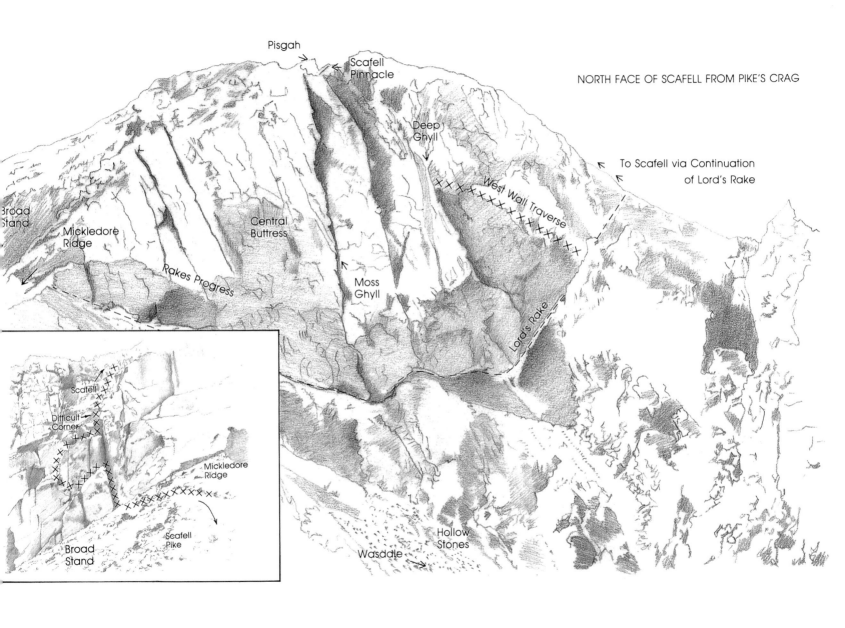

Pisgah

Scafell
Pinnacle

NORTH FACE OF SCAFELL FROM PIKE'S CRAG

Deep
Ghyll

To Scafell via Continuation
of Lord's Rake

West Wall Traverse

Broad
Stand

Mickledore
Ridge

Central
Buttress

Rakes Progress

Moss
Ghyll

Lord's Rake

Scafell

Difficult
Corner

Mickledore
Ridge

Broad
Stand

Scafell
Pike

Hollow
Stones

Wasdale

rediscovered after I had walked back almost to the road. Returning to Borrowdale in the early hours of the morning was a sixty-mile trip by taxi.

However, on a normal day the way is clear and obvious as far as Styhead, with Styhead Tarn sparkling just over the hause, then the path swings south-east and upwards to pass Sprinkling Tarn and below the cliffs of Great End. A last pull upwards takes you to the broad-domed hause with its four-sided windbreak of rocks, near the point where the paths from Allen Crags and Langdale all meet. You are then on the shoulder of the great summit plateau and from then on the well-marked path leads west and then south-west to Calf Cove, where the spring rises that eventually flows into the River Esk. Being the last source of running water, and grass, it was the place where the ponies were tethered in Victorian times when that was the way to climb England's highest mountain. Not all the way though, because from there onwards the way is very rocky indeed, at times over rough boulders, and care may be needed not to sprain an ankle. Even our Victorian forefathers had to walk that stretch, along the main line of the ridge above the cliffs of Broad Crag and Ill Crag, which are not particularly evident from the ridge itself. A brief descent to the hause separating Little Narrowcove from the top of Piers Ghyll is followed by a short climb up the ridge on the other side, and so to the huge cairn on top of Scafell Pike. You've made it!

The path leads fairly obviously from the summit rocks south-west towards Mickledore Ridge (so long as you don't take the Corridor Route in descent by mistake). Unless you intend to go over to Scafell summit, the easiest way down is probably to descend from Mickledore down the earthy gullies and scree below Pikes Crag into the great cirque of Hollowstones. From there the descent to Wasdale Head is straightforwardly down Lingmell Gill.

2a. Reverse of the previous route via Lingmell Spur

The above 'round' can of course be done in reverse, though I would suggest a variation. Walking to Scafell via Brown Tongue and Hollowstones is the way used by rock-climbers and those wishing to get to the high crags quickly. It is certainly direct, because it climbs from the National Trust campsite past Brackenclose (the Fell and Rock Climbing Club hut), up Brown Tongue and into the tremendous combe formed by the cliffs of Scafell and Pike's Crag. (If you should wonder why Brown Tongue is so named, you will wonder no more once you have toiled up it

with a heavy rucksack on a hot summer's day.) Fortunately there is water very high up in Hollowstones and some marvellous summer camping may be had up there.

Instead of panting up Brown Tongue, I would propose as a pleasant change that you head up the grassy spur that Lingmell throws down towards Wastwater. This keeps you on the ridge above the Lingmell gill, leading you up to Goat Crags and, if you choose, to Lingmell Crag itself. The advantage of this route, although it is a little longer, is that – assuming you are aiming to get to Scafell Pike – you can easily see and join the Corridor Route path where it comes over Lingmell Hause and so climb more comfortably to Scafell Pike than is the case via the shale and screes from Hollowstones to Mickledore. To complete the circle, of course, you would head for Esk Hause and return via Styhead.

3. Scafell Pike or Scafell via the Corridor Route

Whereas the Esk Hause route to the main summits curves round the northern end of the massif under Great End and then passes along the main ridge, the Corridor Route heads for the northern end at Styhead then cuts back along the western flank of the mountain. It is an upward-slanting climb and there is a little rocky passage just before the crossing of the top of Greta Gill. The path then passes under the glacier-worn slabs of Round How and across the upper part of Piers Gill – whose deep ravine below is an impressive sight – before climbing up to Lingmell Hause and swinging left up the shoulder to the boulder field on Scafell Pike. It is simple, straightforward and a very good route. The bed of Piers Gill itself, up the watercourse, does provide an exciting way towards Scafell Pike but, although good fun on a hot summer's day, there is one place where there is absolutely no alternative to wading through a pool up to the waist in water, so it is never likely to become popular.

I had a taste of that sort of thing some years ago traversing Crinkle Crags on my own one winter's day when the fells were covered in snow and ice. I crossed a patch of snow that turned out to be the frozen surface of a small but waist deep pool, as I discovered when the ice broke. I immediately retreated and started to run down The Band back to Langdale because the wind was cutting through me like a knife and I was beginning to feel like the famous brass monkey. Even though I did not stop running till I reached Stool End at the bottom of The Band, my breeches were frozen into stiff boards and I was very glad indeed to get them off and into a tracksuit.

Right: Great Gable seen from Lingmell.
Overleaf left: Scafell Pike seen from Foxes Tarn
Overleaf right: From Deep Ghyll (West Wall Traverse) to Mosedale, Pillar and Kirk Fell.

3a. Alternative scrambles on Round How and Broad Crag

Much of the Scafell range is made up of bare rock and is consequently the playground of rock-climbers rather than scramblers. However, good scrambling can be found by leaving the Corridor Route just after it crosses Greta Gill and making a way up the slabs at the far (southern) end of Round How rising in the rocky combe formed between Great End and Broad Crag. As usual, variations are possible, but the main obvious line trends rightwards, crosses an easy terrace, which can provide an escape if wanted, and into a boulder bay. From there it seems best to scramble on to the slabs on the right and so to easier ledges and the top, whence you can start to pick out a line for the next stage.

After a walk into the hollow behind Round How, head for the broken rocks of Broad Crag on the right. Choose a way up the most interesting line of easier rocks – which you will probably find are those up the left side of the continuation of the upper reaches of Piers Gill – and you will shortly arrive on the summit plateau. This line should nowhere be difficult and it is more interesting than the Corridor Route path, which, of course, continues farther and crosses the top of Piers Gill before turning sharply south-east up on to the shoulder of Scafell Pike. It will be fairly obvious, when you are actually there, that there are a few other possible scrambling variations, but resourceful scramblers will not need any lengthy descriptions.

ROUTES FROM ESKDALE

Eskdale is a little more accessible than Wasdale for walkers coming, as most do nowadays, via the main highway of the M6, Kendal Bypass, Windermere and Ambleside. Don't decide to go over the Wrynose and Hardknott passes on a Bank Holiday, because the road between Elterwater and Fellfoot can be entirely blocked with cars in the narrow stretches. Nor should you risk either of them when there is ice on the lower roads. Apart from these exceptions the approach by car – or 'Mountain Goat' – via these high passes is both spectacular and fairly quick. Once in Eskdale, although the approaches to the Scafell range may be a little long, they are worth every drop of sweat. Upper Eskdale in particular is a marvellous place of real mountain grandeur, where the harsh croak of the raven can be heard above the cascading waters of Cam Spout as they foam into the natural basin at its foot; where

the superb architecture of Esk Buttress (called Dow Crag on the O.S. maps, but not by anybody else I think) soars upwards and turns red in the late afternoon light.

In some respects like the upper pastures in the Alps, this high valley of Upper Eskdale somehow always seems a long way from civilisation and something of a sanctuary. In addition, if you leave the Scafells by descending into Upper Eskdale you will find – if you look carefully, just off the path – the finest secluded pools for a quick dip or swim anywhere in the Lake District. Without a doubt the approaches from the south are my favourite ways to reach the Scafells.

4. Scafell via Stony Tarn and Slight Side

From the Woolpack Inn the path climbs north up towards Eel Tarn and then gently leads up to Stony Tarn, before continuing across bouldery ground with a climb up the broad ridge to Slight Side and so on to Scafell. It is straightforward enough and from Slight Side onwards the views are very fine so that the earlier trudge is rewarded.

The last time that I descended this way I was just leaving Slight Side when I watched a solo walker almost tottering up the last slopes to the point where I was having a rest before descending. It was an extremely hot day indeed and I felt quite sorry for him. As he reached me he gasped out 'I don't suppose you have any water?' I told him I was sorry but I wasn't carrying any and was looking forward to a drink from the beck as soon as I reached Upper Eskdale. 'I never drink water from a stream,' he said, in a tone of voice that forbade comment. 'I filled my water bottle from the tap this morning but I have had to drink it all because it is such a hot day. I had no idea that it is such a long way to Scafell.' I didn't really know what to say to him, so made a few more pleasantries and then set off, but I thought to myself that he must have a lot of very thirsty days in the hills if he never has a drink from a stream. I don't normally carry a water bottle at all – there's no need. Perhaps he liked the taste of chlorine?

5. Approaches to Upper Eskdale via the Esk or from Cockley Beck

There are a number of excellent walks and scrambles to be done once you have reached Upper Eskdale – but first you must get that far. There are several possibilities:

Firstly there is the most obvious way, which is to park near the bottom of the Hardknott Pass on the Eskdale side and then walk up the track to Brotherilkeld

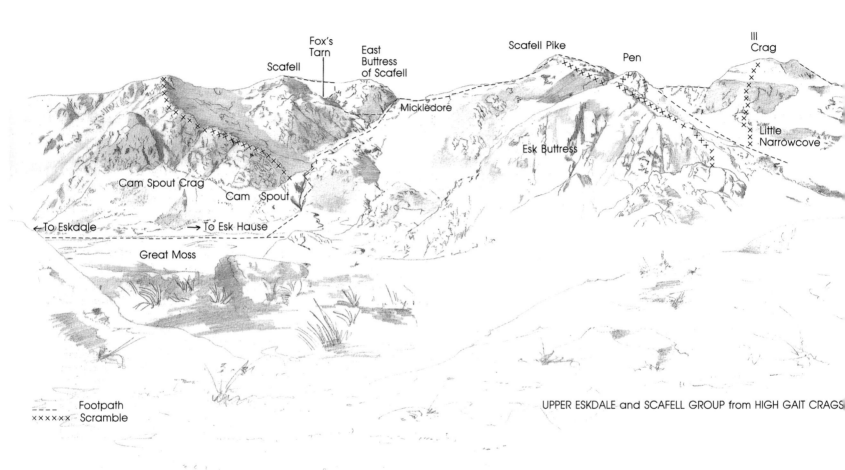

Fox's Tarn

East Buttress of Scafell

Scafell

Scafell Pike

Pen

Ill Crag

Mickledore

Cam Spout Crag

Esk Buttress

Little Narrowcove

Cam Spout

← To Eskdale   → To Esk Hause

Great Moss

– – – – Footpath
×××××× Scramble

UPPER ESKDALE and SCAFELL GROUP from HIGH GAIT CRAGS

Farm. From that point there are three ways from which to choose. Cross the river by the bridge near the farm and follow the footpath until it divides just after crossing Catcove Beck. One way leads steeply uphill for 300 yards and then goes more gently over undulating rocky ground, past Silverybield Crag and High Scarth Crag to reach Cam Spout in Upper Eskdale, having avoided all the lower part of the river. Alternatively, instead of taking the left branch at the fork just after Catcove Beck, you could continue along the north bank of the river, although the path is not so good beyond Heron Crag. Thirdly, the most popular way stays on the south side of the river, heading through fine meadows near the farm – where there is very good camping in summer – and then by stiles and sheepfolds along the generally level valley floor. There are waterfalls at the point where the Lingcove Beck joins the River Esk and the path then climbs steep and somewhat worn grassy slopes rather away from the tumbling river on the left so that the splendid pools for 'skinny dips' can easily be passed unnoticed. Quite suddenly the path reaches more level ground and the Great Moss, which defends Upper Eskdale, must be crossed to approach Cam Spout and enter the sanctuary itself.

There is yet another way, my own favourite, which isn't from Eskdale at all, but from the Duddon Valley. One of its great advantages is that there is no need to drive over the scary hairpins of Hardknott, for there is good parking a couple of hundred yards after the cattle grid at Cockley Beck bridge, just before the road begins its climb upwards at the bottom of Border End. The way then heads north up the left bank of Mosedale Beck but after a mile it becomes rather boggy. It is nowhere near as bad as the 'Bostik Trots' of the Pennine Way, but it is very wet just the same. With experience it is much better, but walkers on a first visit may be seen leaping like goats from rock to rock trying to avoid wet feet.

The cliffs of the Scafell group peep tantalisingly, but distantly, in front. Beyond the hause ahead a short descent leads to the Lingcove Beck running down from Bowfell to join the River Esk. Rather disconcertingly the path, which was obvious enough, disappears. It would be more accurate to say that it joins up with the path coming from Eskdale and heading for the Ore Gap, but that isn't the way to go to reach Upper Eskdale. A couple more leaps to cross the Lingcove Beck (plenty of good boulders) and you will be able to head north-west along sheep tracks which wind up over and between various rocky outcrops (Long Crags, Low Gait Crag and High Gait Crags) – and there is the Great Moss at last. Its

eastern edge should be skirted on the drier rocky ground, but unless you are going to tramp a long way up Upper Eskdale you are probably going to get wet feet picking your way cautiously across the Great Moss to the firm ground below the ramparts of Cam Spout Crag and Esk Buttress.

Have a drink and a snack below the crags, for you are in one of the finest amphitheatres in the Lake District with a choice of marvellous walks, scrambles or climbs before you.

6. Footpaths to the Scafells from Upper Eskdale

The map shows two footpaths from Upper Eskdale leading on to the Scafell summits.

6a. Via Cam Spout to Mickledore

The south-westerly path, to your left as you look at the line of cliffs from below Esk Buttress, goes up the right bank of the How Beck as it tumbles down the combe, with a splendid waterfall – Cam Spout – at its base. The path follows easy-angled rocks, which are much easier going up than down, and then passes right underneath the crags of the East Buttress of Scafell to attain the Mickledore Ridge. It is a climb of about two thousand feet, an attractive way and fairly well used, and the presence of the stream makes it easily located in mist.

6b. Via Little Narrowcove

The second path shown on the map reaches the main Great End–Scafell ridge up the broad gully of Little Narrowcove, which separates the great rock masses of Ill Crag and Esk Buttress (Dow Crag). Again the tumbling beck aids location in mist, but it is best reserved as a way of ascent suitable for emergency use only, such as when the weather is particularly bad or foggy.

There are at least three other ways out of the amphitheatre that are much more interesting. They are however neither well-marked nor easy-angled and they will not appeal to fell-walkers who want to stay on obvious footpaths.

6c. Scramble to Scafell Pike via Pen

The first of these ways, and my own favourite, involves walking up Upper Eskdale to just beyond Esk Buttress. By striking up the fellside before you reach the bottom of Little Narrowcove, you may pick a way up grassy ledges and rocky shelves to scramble up splendidly rough rock to the quite distinct summit of Pen, which is directly behind Esk Buttress. It is possible to make this early section rather harder by scrambling up steeper rock near Thor's Cave (an obvious dark slit just beyond Esk Buttress), but for a solo scrambler it is better to start a little farther right, where it is easier. I won't pretend that the early scrabbling about immediately after you have left the main path is particularly enjoyable, but it is this part of the way that deters the hordes and means that you can enjoy being on Pen on your own. Because it is surrounded by so many great buttresses and crags, this fine little summit is itself often overlooked by climbers who are intent on greater deeds on Esk Buttress or the East Buttress of Scafell.

The final pyramid is superb rock and a marvellous scramble to its top is feasible almost anywhere, though it is easiest towards the left side. Beyond the summit of Pen a broad rock ridge stretches away, with one band of steeper rock barring the way forward. Again the easiest way is to the left, or a good scramble can be had by trending farther right. Beyond this is a stonefield and then another little ridge leads without difficulty to the Eskdale cairn which is only a few yards from the actual summit of Scafell Pike. It is a worthy approach to England's highest mountain and, even if there are three hundred people above, you will neither hear nor see them until you reach the summit.

6d. Scramble to Scafell via the edge of Cam Spout Crag

My second unmarked-on-the-map way up is nearly as good, though I think it is better as a descent from Scafell rather than as an ascent.

As you sit having your sandwiches somewhere below Esk Buttress, let your eye search out where Cam Spout pours down the slabby rocks. You will also see where a rock ridge curves down into the amphitheatre and to some extent forms the northern edge of Cam Spout Crags. The route follows the ridge. As with Pen the initial bit of the approach is the least attractive part, because it is across rough ground with hardly a sheep track to help. Once attained, however, the ridge becomes more defined and by the time you have climbed to reach the main ridge it is quite narrow. As a way of descending into Upper Eskdale, particularly if you have had a long day on the Scafells from the Duddon Valley approach (Cockley Beck), it is the best way

there is, because it is steep but not hard going. You also arrive in just the right place to cross Great Moss and return to the head of Mosedale. There are good views across the amphitheatre and to Pen, for once seen standing out from its neighbours.

In mist it is not so easy to locate, and a combination of map, compass, watch and altimeter may prove useful. Incidentally, while the use of a map and compass in the mountains should be obvious, as also the use of a watch to estimate distance covered in mist, the use of an altimeter may seem less so. I started using an altimeter for ski-touring in the Alps some years ago but have found that its use extends successfully to the British hills. However, technology moves on: nowadays, global satellite tracking and the GPS can pinpoint your position to within ten metres.

6e. Scramble to Scafell Pike via Ill Crag

This time it is up, through and over the slabs and ribs of rock that buttress Ill Crag. There is a 'recommended' route which you may follow to surmount this great mass of rock and steep grass which makes up the right wall of Little Narrowcove, but I have to admit that, although I have tried to find it on three occasions, I am sure that I have myself not yet found it. Basically, of course, the best scrambling routes find a line up the most continuous bits of clean rock, and each time I have found a different one and all varying in difficulty. It was, however, enjoyable each time, and it surely does not matter whether one sticks to, or even finds, the 'best' line. Almost in any direction there is an exhilarating scramble and you emerge on the summit ridge with the distinct feeling of climbing on ground that has never before had a human footprint. Once on the summit ridge Scafell Pike is near by and you can either head north towards Esk Hause to descend, continue the circuit round to Scafell Pike, or scuttle down little Narrowcove back into Upper Eskdale.

If the Ill Crag face seems a little daunting, you may always go a little farther up Upper Eskdale and, leaving the face on your left, work out a pleasant scramble-walk up the broken Cockly Pike ridge which also leads to the summit of Ill Crag.

Probably the most enjoyable round incorporating the best of these scrambles is to climb to Scafell Pike from Pen, cross Mickledore Ridge and climb to Scafell – either via Broad Stand or Foxes Tarn – then descend the ridge towards Slight Side. Return to Upper Eskdale by way of the curving ridge at the edge of Cam Spout Crags. It's a marvellous day.

Cam Spout Crags and Scafell seen across the Great Moss.

ROUTES FROM BORROWDALE

7. Scafell Pike or Scafell via Styhead Gill

Two obvious valleys descend northwards from the massif near Great End and both start at the friendly little hamlet of Seathwaite, where many cars can be found parked over the weekend while their owners tramp the high fells. These two valleys contain Styhead Gill on the one hand and Ruddy Gill joining Grains Gill on the other. The main bridle-way is up Styhead Gill so go due south straight out of Seathwaite up the left bank of the beck and then swing right at Stockley Bridge to climb the slopes of Aaron Crags. Eventually you will arrive on the breast of the fell just above the point where Taylorgill Force – whose position you can guess at but not see – tumbles away with a great splash. A half-mile tramp up the bank of the stream follows to reach Styhead Tarn and a welcome rest at the mountain-rescue box at Styhead. There is then a choice of routes up to Scafell Pike, just as if you had reached this point from Wasdale, which will include the Corridor Route or heading uphill past Sprinkling Tarn to Esk Hause.

7a. The Scafells via Grains Gill with optional scramble en route in Ruddy Gill

There is a more direct way to Esk Hause and the Scafells, with the additional option of an interesting and enjoyable scramble alongside the path. Immediately after crossing Stockley Bridge, instead of going rightwards for Styhead, turn left up Grains Gill.

Enthusiasts will start their scrambling by entering the broad and bouldery ravine of Grains Gill itself by descending to the left from the main path when a footbridge is seen below and a tumbledown wall is ahead. A point will be reached where the waters of Ruddy Gill join Grains Gill in an attractive cascade and rock steps can be climbed on its right-hand side. Clean rock slabs and a series of pools and waterfalls follow until it is advisable to leave the gill at a difficult bit. The gill can be rejoined before ending at the point where the main path crosses Ruddy Gill at a footbridge.

The path continues up the left bank but there is pleasant and easy walking and scrambling up the clean rocks in the stream bed for a couple of hundred yards to an open bouldery stretch. It is then advisable to join the path again until the upper ravine is reached. The path climbs to the left but scramblers may enjoy gaining height by following the ravine itself. The scrambling is in fact very straightforward for quite a way until it is unfortunately ended at a narrow pool with a vertical left wall, a very steep right wall and a lively cascade blocking the exit. Very adventurous scramblers may try the right wall and succeed but most will prefer to retreat a little, escape to the path for a little way and rejoin the gill higher up. A little more scrambling then remains until a final pool blocks progress and an exit can be made to the shelf immediately below the impressive cliffs of Great End.

I saw them for the first time at the age of seventeen and, having in my possession my first ice axe and crampons, I wanted desperately to climb the Great Gully. There was good snow in the gullies and after a hard frost it was a brilliant day with the sun sparkling appealingly high above on the rime of the upper cliff. We had a marvellous day chopping steps up the icy bulge in the middle and burrowing right through the cornice at the top of the gully, Much later, that evening, while walking down the road from Seathwaite I still had icicles hanging from my eyebrows and woolly hat. I've been on Great End several times since then – on one memorable occasion being followed almost half-way up by one of my dogs without my noticing he was there. As on other occasions he was shoved unceremoniously into my rucksack and finished the route in relative comfort.

Once you have arrived under the Great End cliffs you have joined the 'trade route' from Langdale and it is a straightforward gentle climb up to what is generally (if erroneously) called Esk Hause, before swinging round to the west up the main path towards Scafell Pike. Alternatively you may climb from below Great End up a slightly steeper path which cuts off the corner to reach the same path to Scafell. If you have time and inclination it is well worth while detouring a little to enjoy the views from the top of the Great End cliffs, for these are not only very fine but you will find yourself on a less popular path along the heights of the main ridge. Descend from Scafell Pike by the Corridor Route as far as Styhead Tarn but, if mist comes down while you are clambering about on Scafell Pike, take particular care in finding the correct line from the summit cairn. If in doubt, return to the summit and then make your way back down the last little spur that you recently clambered up – from the dip in the ridge at the top of Little Narrowcove – and it is then a steep but easy descent down shale and scree to the north-west, with a stepped path at its bottom. You will soon cross the

Great Gable and Green Gable seen from near the head of Ruddy Gill.

55

Corridor Route path and can turn right along it in certainty to reach Styhead. The main path down Aaron Crags back to Stockley Bridge is no more pleasant in descent than on the way up, for it is eroded and rocky. Better to finish a grand day by crossing instead to the left bank of the Styhead Beck well above Taylorgill Force. The path clings somewhat precariously to the hillside, giving a fine view of the waterfall, picking a way over jutting craglets and tree-roots and finally nipping down through the fields to finish through the archway in the farm buildings at Seathwaite.

8. The Eskdale Round

Before leaving the Scafell range I would not like to miss out a splendid though strenuous walk: the Eskdale Round. It cannot normally be considered a winter walk, because it is rather long for the available daylight at that time of year, but as a challenging walk for those who are fit it is well worth doing. A good starting point is Brotherilkeld, at the foot of the Hardknott Pass, then by way of High Scarth Crag to Slight Side and so on to Scafell. The experience and competence of the party will influence the choice of way from Scafell to Scafell Pike, after which you take the stony path to Esk Hause, go over to Esk Pike and then head for Bowfell. You may make an escape by descending from the Ore Gap down Yeastyrigg Gill and so to the Lingcove Beck and Eskdale, but you should traverse Bowfell as far as Three Tarns – from that point also an escape can be made if desired. The last major group to be crossed is then the Crinkles. I have found ways off the Crinkles down Long Top to Lingcove Beck, in order to get back to Eskdale without having to tramp over Hardknott Pass. However, if you resolve that the crossing of Hardknott holds no terrors for you at the end of this long day – or you've been far-sighted enough to arrange your transport back over the

pass in advance – you will want to continue your line south along the ridge beyond the Crinkles and descend the fellside from Little Stand to Cockley Beck.

I once went on this round with a party of friends on a summer's day which started well but turned misty, cold and into a real downpour just as we reached Scafell. Having descended Broad Stand safely we were strung out rather badly on the stretch to Esk Hause and so decided to split into two groups, the faster one to walk down Upper Eskdale to Brotherilkeld. The plan was sound enough but of course it didn't work out as planned. The slower party headed off for Eskdale from Esk Hause, in thick mist and rain. Many hours later, having rationalised all the way down that either their compass was faulty, or that the rocks were obviously magnetic, or that the large rock that they spotted looming out of the mist was the one they had seen much earlier, they arrived – at Rosthwaite in Borrowdale! They had headed off from Esk Hause in exactly the wrong direction and gone down Langstrath. They were of course eventually rescued.

9. The Wasdale Screes

As a final word before leaving the Scafell Group I feel it must be appropriate to mention the Wasdale Screes. They don't apparently suit a circular walk – unless you intend to get involved in a major effort such as the traverse of all the peaks around Wasdale – but they can give a surprisingly scenic one. Walk from Brackenclose (at the head of the lake) over Illgill Head and along the tops of The Screes. Farther south, just beyond the high point of Whin Rigg, watch for the curious defile of Greathall Gill running down towards the foot of Wastwater. A path leads down there which enables you to pick up one traversing the foot of the impressive Screes and so back to base, while admiring the great peaks at the head of Wasdale all clustered together to great scenic advantage.

Scafell Pike, Esk Buttress, Pen and Ill Crag seen across Upper Eskdale.

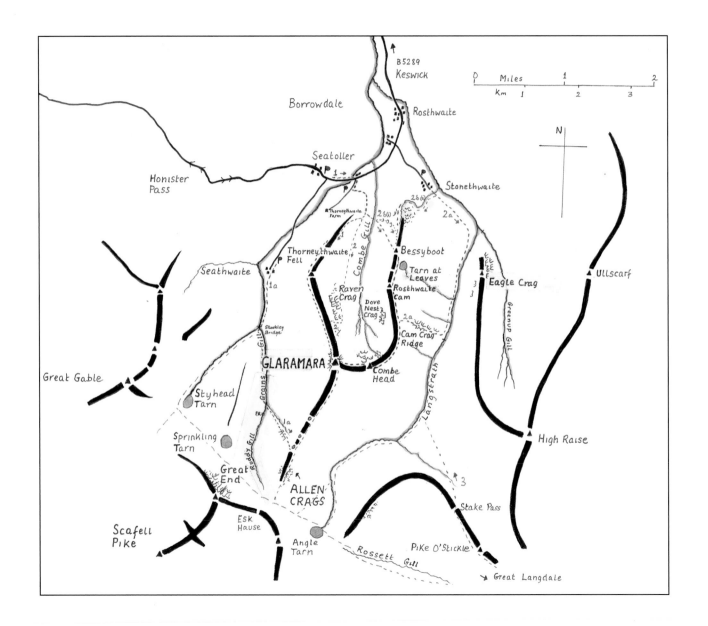

THE GLARAMARA and ALLEN CRAGS GROUP

	Approximate Time	Star Rating	Assessment of Difficulty
1. Glaramara and Allen Crags from Borrowdale via Thorneythwaite Fell	5–7 hours	*	—
1a. Glaramara or Allen Crags: scrambling route via Grains Gill	add 1 hours	**	1–2
2. Glaramara via Raven Crag, Combe Gill	3–4 hours	*	1
2a. Glaramara from Langstrath via Cam Crag Ridge with optional scramble	5–7 hours	***	2
2b. Two approaches to Glaramara via Bessyboot, with optional scramble on Intake Ridge	4–5 hours	*	2–3
3. Langdale to Borrowdale, with scrambles on Middlefell, Loft Crag, Cam Crag Ridge and Raven Crag (or 'Corvus')	8–12 hours	***	3

GLARAMARA and ALLEN CRAGS GROUP

To any reader of the classic Herries Chronicles of Hugh Walpole – based as they are on Borrowdale – the name of Glaramara must surely strike an echo of adventure and romance, and in truth it doesn't disappoint. The main footpath to Glaramara starts from near Seatoller and gives a very satisfactory outing via its north ridge, but there are also other possibilities of outstanding merit. As there are only a few peaks it is difficult to call this a 'group' but nevertheless it is distinctly isolated from the Gables by Grains Gill and from the Langdale Pikes by the long Langstrath. Glaramara has two summits while there are four along the broad ridge that joins Glaramara to Allen Crags, and the walking and scrambling possibilities in this small area are much better than a cursory inspection would suggest. The most obvious route is along the main ridge so let's start with that.

1. Glaramara and Allen Crags from Borrowdale via Thorneythwaite Fell

Wherever you park (Rosthwaite, Seatoller, or off the road between them) turn down the track heading for Thorneythwaite Farm. This leaves the road at Strands Bridge, opposite the houses of Mountain View. Access to the fell is then via a stile and gate on the left, only fifty yards along this track (where there are also some parking possibilities a few yards farther on). Across sparsely-wooded fields the path joins a stony track emerging from Combe Gill, with the torrent rushing below through a wooded gorge. A kissing gate in the intake wall leads to the open fell. For many years there used to be a notice here warning of the dangerous condition of the caves of Dovenest Crag, which lies ahead in the combe, but it has now disappeared and rock-climbers seem to frequent the crags again.

Shortly after the gate the path turns uphill and a minor path forks left, on the level. Stay with the main path, which soon climbs and twists steadily upwards on to Thorneythwaite Fell but generally follows the north ridge of Glaramara. Some stretches of peaty ground are crossed before the final rocks of Glaramara rear up ahead.

A short scramble up a rocky gully (unusual for the Lakeland fells) leads to one of Glaramara's twin summits. The other summit is only a short scramble away so you can enjoy the best of both worlds by having half of your sandwiches admiring Borrowdale and the other half looking across to the Langdale Pikes beyond Langstrath.

We once climbed Glaramara on a misty, dark and cheerless day in January. There had been many such days already that month and, to tell the truth, we really only went up for the exercise. Surprisingly, however, as we climbed the last rocks to the first summit, we suddenly emerged above the mist and were bathed in gloriously brilliant sunshine. Great Gable stood out of a blanket of cloud, sparkling with new snow, as did the Langdale Pikes and Allen Crags ahead. It was a truly magical sight.

Originally we had only intended to climb Glaramara and then return, but because the sun was shining in this beautiful world above the dank clouds we walked the whole length of the ridge to Allen Crags and then Esk Hause. Very reluctantly we only descended into the fog again as we were obliged to lose altitude beyond Angle Tarn on the way down to the rough track at the head of Langstrath. Of course, in addition to the fog, the fact that it was nearly five o'clock on a January afternoon also meant that it was soon dark. Consequently we had the doubtful pleasure of stumbling down not only a rocky but also a very boggy track. Frustratingly we only had one head-torch amongst the four of us, which greatly complicated the descent. For years afterwards my wife remembered all the trials and tribulations of that descent but I must admit that I had entirely forgotten them. I remembered only the marvellous views, and the annoying fact that I had failed to take my camera. Cloud inversions like that are a rarity.

I should mention that the broad ridge running from Glaramara to the point where you peer over to Esk Hause is nearly two miles long and with a lot more undulations and bends in the path than you might expect. Three small tarns, one after the other in rocky hollows, can prove very useful in establishing your precise position in a mist. After the last climb up to Allen Crags and the short descent to Esk Hause a return can be made either down Langstrath or Grains Gill.

1a. Glaramara or Allen Crags: scrambling route via Grains Gill

This is an excellent scrambling way to the main Glaramara–Allen Crags ridge as it is an unexpectedly interesting approach, with delightful and varied scenery. There are few difficulties, though the scrambling on the high crags at the end of this course is open and fairly exposed, but fortunately there are excellent holds. A reasonably dry spell will give the best conditions.

Start from Seathwaite (where there is plenty of roadside parking) and walk up the main highway towards Styhead. At Stockley Bridge (where the routes diverge) turn left immediately and follow the good path up the right-hand side of Grains Gill towards the point where the stream forks. Just before reaching the fork, descend into the ravine on the left. At first it is wide and boulder-strewn, but the main water flow is from Ruddy Gill, coming in from the right, so the flow noticeably decreases as you progress, while the ravine is narrower. Soon the stream swings left, where it has cut a channel down a thin vein of creamy-white quartz and this can be climbed to a series of rock steps, leading upwards for some distance to a wider and more bouldery section. Now follow the stream, or its left bank, until it bends to the left between two rowans.

A long and delightful section of scrambling then leads up the clean rocks of the streambed, with little cascades and steps of rock, until a steep-sided ravine below beetling crags is reached. The ravine is much more difficult than anything lower down and it is advisable to escape to the left bank on rock and grass until you can cross to an obvious rib of clean rock below a prominent buttress on the right. On reaching the buttress scramble up a left-slanting groove at its foot on good holds until it seems wiser to head back right to easier-angled rocks on the crest.

The rock is excellent so go straight up on fine holds until the angle eases again. Ahead is a sharp prow of obviously difficult rock, but to the immediate left of the prow there is a staircase of ledges and 'jug handle' holds, which lead very easily, though in an exposed position, to the crest of the ridge again. It is then easy walking over rocky ground to the main footpath which links Allen Crags to Glaramara. Either head leftwards over the broad fell to Glaramara or, of course, rightwards to Allen Crags.

If you choose Glaramara you may descend from its summit down Thorneythwaite Fell towards Rosthwaite and then follow the footpath leading back towards Seathwaite. Alternatively, you may descend much more directly but very steeply down the cairned fellside to Seathwaite. For those who choose Allen Crags at the end of the scrambling, the return may be made down Langstrath from Angle Tarn or by the easier way via Sprinkling Tarn, Styhead Tarn and Styhead Gill.

2. Glaramara via Raven Crag, Combe Gill

This is an interesting variation on the previously described north ridge route which also gives a pleasant and easy scramble.

Shortly after leaving the fell gate, instead of following the main path rising to Thorneythwaite Crag, take the level one leading into the combe. This path, sometimes faint, crosses a few boggy stretches then rises towards Raven Crag, seen

ahead on the right, eventually skirting the base of its steep rocks. This path is almost certainly kept open mainly by climbers heading for the ever-popular rock-climb of 'Corvus'. This has been known for years as the best 'Diff.' in the Lakes, but nowadays its true grading on some particularly polished pitches is probably 'V. Diff.' It is popular with many walkers who are also rock-climbers – and rightly so, especially as part of a varied day on these grand fells.

Beyond the base of the main crags the path fades away, but a short, steeper rise up rockier and wetter ground leads to a long rake rising diagonally rightwards, with a retaining wall on its right side. When the wall comes to an end (shortly beyond the point where 'Corvus' also finishes) either continue in the same line to the top of the gully seen ahead and escape up the left side of that, or else trend leftwards up steep slopes to reach the grassy moor beyond. From here strike west and the path to Glaramara's summits is easily joined.

2a. Glaramara from Langstrath via Cam Crag Ridge with optional scramble

I spent many blinkered years looking at the Lakeland hills without realising how much additional enjoyment and interest is to be found on many of the easy-angled crags and rocky slopes. One of the very best of these is Cam Crag Ridge in Langstrath. Undoubtedly I must have seen it long before I first became aware of it, but it was only when I read about it in one of Harry Griffin's enthusiastic books that I decided to explore the ridge myself.

The beauty of Cam Crag Ridge is that you can make its ascent as hard or as easy as you like. Walkers will stick to the slanting rakes and easy ledges, scramblers will find steeper rock up which to find a way, while even rock-climbers may find a few pitches of interest. Essentially one seeks out one's own way up almost a thousand feet of rock, which is laid back in little slabs and walls that are to a great extent mainly bare of vegetation. Where the rock steepens, easy rakes can be found to avoid difficulties, so that even under adverse conditions the ascent can give pleasure.

In many respects Cam Crag must now be very much the same as when the ice scraped it bare and bony long ago. Those who seek it out will find it more reminiscent of a bit of Sutherland in Scotland than part of the Lake District. Amazingly few people seem to have realised that the crag is there and there is still only the very faintest of paths to its foot. Go and climb it when there are juicy bilberries ripe for picking and the odds are still that there will only be you and your friends in sight.

The approach is by walking up Langstrath from Rosthwaite and, after leaving the junction with Greenup Gill, you must go at least a mile up the valley. You may arrive at a narrow wooden bridge spanning the river at a place where it runs through a rocky gorge. If you reach that point you have gone too far. Turn around and look behind. Cam Crag Ridge, with a pile of huge boulders at its foot, will then be apparent directly in front of you. The hillside up to the boulders is a bit of a struggle and, despite the fact you may think that the boulders will block access to the ridge, they can easily be circumvented on their left. Thereafter it is delightful scrambling with a choice of difficulty for all tastes and you will thoroughly enjoy yourself.

When you reach the top of the ridge it is probably best to keep going over rocky lumps and bumps until you realise that you are looking over the head of Combe Gill and facing you is Raven Crag. Either make your way over Combe Head to reach Glaramara and then go back down Thorneythwaite Fell or find your way to Tarn at Leaves where a cairned path leads back down towards Borrowdale. By the latter route you will, of course, reach the torrent flowing from Combe Gill near the intake wall and will need to cross it. Although in dry weather this is easy enough, in winter conditions it may be impossible. In this event do not attempt the crossing, but stay on the right-hand bank and follow a stony path north-east towards Stonethwaite. You will soon spot a bridge and public footpath leading back to the road just east of Mountain View.

What more can I say but 'Go and do this truly marvellous ridge.' You won't be disappointed as it is undoubtedly one of the very best Lakeland scramble-walks.

2b. Two approaches to Glaramara via Bessyboot, with optional scramble on Intake Ridge

The stretch of fell country between Langstrath Beck and Combe Gill is one of the least-visited corners of the Lake District. Certainly, the few paths across it are more sheep tracks than anything else and it is only the appearance of the odd rock cairn here and there which convinces you that yours are not the first human feet to tread that particular ground. Its rocky wilderness is very attractive and set amongst it is a sharp little summit with the curious name of Bessyboot. This stands proudly above a lonely sheet of water having the equally intriguing name of Tarn at Leaves. What sort of leaves they may have been must be sought in your imagination, for there isn't a tree in sight.

Combe Head and Raven Crag from near Rosthwaite Cam.

For the first of these ways to Bessyboot, from the Thorneythwaite Farm track (see 1.), walk up to the entrance to Combe Gill but, as soon as you have passed through the fell gate drop down to the beck and use the large boulders to cross to the east bank. Thereafter a faint path slants upwards to the south-east, between Rottenstones Gill on the right and rockier slopes on the left, while occasional reassuring cairns confirm that your navigational skills are not lost. (Incidentally, if you find this slope a bit tough, consider the runners in the Borrowdale Fell Race; they have taken to using this path on the way to Glaramara, before they continue to Scafell, Great Gable, Brandreth, Honister and Dale Head.) Tarn at Leaves and Bessyboot, above it on the left, are soon located.

The second approach to Bessyboot is one with which I was not familiar when I first wrote this book. It is very good, even dramatic, although with a very steep start which has the merit of gaining height quickly. For this, walk through the hamlet of Stonethwaite, past the hotel and along the lane beyond until you are directly opposite the point where this has an entrance into the campsite. Here, turn off right through a gate and head up the slope beyond. Although not immediately apparent, a path soon appears, leading steeply uphill through trees up the edge of Big Stanger Gill, with an impressive ravine on the right-hand side. A series of made steps lead to a ladder-stile over what would have otherwise have been an awkward wall, to a slight descent into the head of the gill, then rising to a point where the now quieter stream is easily crossed on to boggier but more level ground. Follow its general course westwards towards various rocky tops seen ahead, veering leftwards as you near them and Bessyboot will soon be located, as it is the only one with a clear path up it. It is an excellent viewpoint.

After reaching Bessyboot and Tarn at Leaves, the next objective, upwards and to the south across rough ground, is the sharp rock spike of Rosthwaite Cam, which, once attained, gives fine retrospective views. From here it is difficult to say, 'Now follow the crest of the ridge,' for the jumble of rocky eminences and grassy swellings ahead hardly qualify as such. Paths start and disappear again just as quickly but there is no difficulty in moving steadily higher until you reach the rocky gateway at the head of Combe Gill. Steeper rocks then rear up on the right, defending access to the heights of Combe Head, beyond which lies the summit of Glaramara. If you are feeling courageous these rocks can yield a good scramble, but more prudent souls will pass through the 'gate' and find an easier slope on the far side of Combe Head.

Beyond, a traverse across a boggy hollow, usually containing a small tarn or two, leads easily to the footpath which rises up to the summits of Glaramara. The return to Borrowdale over Thorneythwaite Fell is via a good footpath, which should be obvious on most occasions.

An optional start to the walk just described could incorporate a well-known scramble on the so-called Intake Ridge. Until you start looking for it you could easily doubt its existence, but this 'ridge' links together a series of fairly isolated buttresses of clean rock that provide an enjoyable alternative to the faint path up to Tarn at Leaves. To find it you must first pass through the fell gate at the entrance to Combe Gill then descend to the beck, which must be forded. Then follow the intake wall on the other side of the stream over a boulder field until it ends against rocky buttresses that run down the hillside.

Although I can tell you that this is the point to start scrambling I can't tell you exactly where to go, for I never seem to have done it twice in the same way. There is at least one 'semi-official' description of the route but you should opt for your own personal level of difficulty. The line deteriorates towards the top, particularly after a good rock wall at mid-height has been overcome, but overall it is pleasant and the views of the cultivated fields and tree-girt crags of Borrowdale below are very fine. After only a short distance the rocky little summit of Bessyboot is soon reached.

3. Langdale to Borrowdale, with scrambles on Middlefell, Loft Crag, Cam Crag Ridge and Raven Crag (or 'Corvus')

Just one final suggestion for a day covering some of the best bits of this area. You will need to be feeling particularly energetic and prepared to get cracking early because this is a long haul.

Start in Langdale with an ascent of Middlefell Buttress above the Old Dungeon Ghyll, or take the easier scramble up the side of Raven Crag. Continue scrambling up Loft Crag on the way to Pike o' Stickle then head over to the top of the Stake Pass. Cam Crag Ridge is clearly visible and beckoning from this point, and will be a delight in the late morning sunshine. Finish it all off by descending into Combe Gill and either climb 'Corvus' on Raven Crag or scramble up the rocky terrace on its left-hand side in order to attain Glaramara. All that remains is to return to Langdale by way of Allen Crags, Esk Hause and Rossett Gill. It is highly likely that you'll be fairly weary as you trudge down the valley for a welcome drink – but very satisfied after such a day.

Tarn at Leaves from Bessyboot.

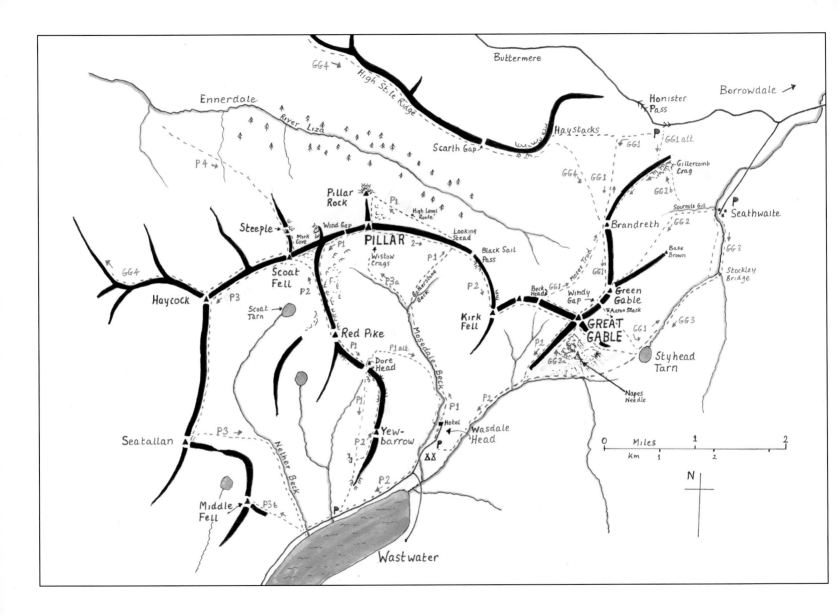

PILLAR and GREAT GABLE GROUP

	Approximate Time	Rating	Assessment of Difficulty
PILLAR SECTION			
1. The High Level Route to Pillar Rock and Pillar, Steeple, Red Pike and Dore Head	5–7 hours	***	—
1a. Optional scramble: the 'Slab and Notch' route	add 1/2 hour	***	3
2. The Greater Mosedale Round: Yewbarrow, Red Pike, Pillar, Kirk Fell, Great Gable	6–8 hours	***	—
3. Pillar via Looking Stead, Scoat Fell, Haycock and Seatallan	5–6 hours	**	—
3a. Alternative scramble to Pillar via Wistow Crags	add 1 hour	***	2–3
3b. The main walk in reverse, with alternative scramble start on Middlefell	add 1 hour	*	2–3
4. Pillar: routes from Ennerdale	variable	—	—
GREAT GABLE SECTION			
1. Great Gable from Honister via Brandreth and Green Gable; return via Beck Head and Moses' Trod	4–6 hours	**	—
2. Great Gable from Seathwaite in Borrowdale	4–6 hours	**	—
2a. Alternative scramble in Sourmilk Gill	add 3/4 hour	**	2
2b. Alternative scramble on Gillercomb Crag	add 1–11/2 hours	**	2
3. Great Gable by the 'Climber's Traverse'	5–6 hours	•••	1
3a. Optional scrambles:			
'Threading the Needle'	10 minutes	—	
Via Sphinx Ridge	3/4 hour	—	
On Westmorland Crags	1/2 hour	••	2–3
4. The Ennerdale Horseshoe	10–12 hours	•••	—

PILLAR and GREAT GABLE GROUP

This wonderful and awe-inspiring group of mountains clustered round the head of Wasdale needs little recommendation. Yewbarrow, Kirkfell, Great Gable and Pillar in particular provide some of the grandest scenery and mountain-walking in the Lake District and are well worth the extra little effort needed to get to them.

For Pillar, Wasdale Head is the best base, while Wasdale Head, Seathwaite in Borrowdale, or the top of Honister Pass, are all reasonable access points for Great Gable.

PILLAR SECTION

1. The High Level Route to Pillar Rock and Pillar, Steeple, Red Pike and Dore Head

The broad, stony dome of Pillar mountain is almost flat and it doesn't have many of the normal vertical attributes of a pillar at all. The glory of this fine mountain is of course the great buttress of Pillar Rock overlooking Ennerdale, which more than compensates for any deficiencies of its parent. For about a century successive waves of rock-climbers have sought newer and harder routes on Pillar Rock, while its soaring architecture and comparative isolation, by Lake District standards, have always made it a very special place to visit. I have happy memories of sunny weekends camping just below and rock-climbing on Pillar Rock, and a friend told me how he once sat, like a sailor in a crow's nest, on top of High Man on the Rock for half an hour in a howling gale of wind and rain and felt very contented. It is a most impressive piece of rock with an atmosphere of its own and there can be little doubt that to arrive by the High Level Route is so satisfying that any other approach would seem an anticlimax by comparison, particularly for a first-time visitor.

Start at Wasdale Head, where there is plenty of parking space on the green, just before reaching the Wastwater Head Inn, then go north up the right-hand side of Mosedale following the line of the Gatherstone Beck towards the Black Sail Pass and Ennerdale. Shortly after the path crosses the beck, you may choose to take a fainter path slanting in a more direct line towards the rocks of Looking Stead, which cuts off quite a corner. As you may guess, it is steeper. From near the top of the pass the path swings west over the rocky lump of Looking Stead on the crest of the ridge, to reach a cairn just after a level section, just beyond the last of some iron fence posts and at the beginning of a steep rise. A path branches to the right, descends slightly at first and then traverses the steep mountainside above Ennerdale. This is the High Level Route to Pillar Rock, and it is one of the most spectacular, easy walks in the Lake District.

Follow the path for about three quarters of a mile until Robinson's Cairn is reached and revel in the sudden, superb view of the East Face of Pillar Rock. Robinson's Cairn was blown up some years ago by extremists protesting about something or other. It was soon afterwards rebuilt and continues to commemorate the hardy John Wilson Robinson, who climbed the great rock over a hundred times and who, incidentally, was with Professor Norman Collie when the 'Collie Step' on Scafell was chipped in the rock with an ice axe. (Other loonies blew up the cairns on Ill Bell, Kentmere, but they were also replaced.

A path heads for the base of the Rock but unless you are going rock-climbing on the West Face it is best avoided since, after crossing the awkward bit in the gully, you will merely have a nasty scramble up loose scree and arrive by a much longer and less satisfactory way at the Jordan Gap. The normal route goes there by a much more well-worn path that slants across a rocky shelf above the crags of the Shamrock, scrambling up and across well-marked rocks to reach the rocky lump of Pisgah. This is a little lower than the main high point, High Man, and to its left, separated from it by the Jordan Gap. (On the right of High Man and at a lower level is the rock platform of Low Man.) The main path continues from the neck which joins Pisgah to the mountain and then heads steeply upwards on stony ground to the summit of Pillar a few hundred feet higher.

I have very clear memories of how steep that last pull up to Pillar can seem for it was near the end of one of my best ever mountain days. We started at 4 a.m. in Langdale and firstly went up The Band and climbed Bowfell Buttress by the normal route. We then walked over Esk Pike to Scafell, climbed Scafell Pinnacle and descended the Corridor Route to Styhead. Continuing what developed into a very full day we walked to Great Gable and climbed Needle Ridge, then trudged wearily over Kirk Fell to Black Sail Pass, and by the High Level Route to Pillar Rock. There we climbed the New West Route and arrived eventually at the Jordan Gap in a state of collapse. We then had to totter to the

Great Gable from Down in the Dale Bridge.

top of Pillar and descend Wind Gap to Wasdale Head. One or two very fit members of the party, not content with all that, carried on to do the rest of the Mosedale round and were still back before I had finished.

1a. Optional scramble: the 'Slab and Notch' route

While in the area and going past Pillar Rock, I must mention the excellent little scramble called the 'Slab and Notch' route to the summit of High Man. Just before the main path reaches Pisgah, another little track branches right at a cairn to traverse the broken lower rocks of Pisgah and into a gully below the Jordan Gap. The Slab of the route should be obvious, inclining gently downwards and well marked, just to the right of the gully. From the gully easy steps lead up on to the slab, then a step down to a horizontal ledge leads right then upwards again on good holds to the Notch, which is just a gap in the ridge. From the Notch another ledge leads right to more good holds up another little ridge; an obvious track heads for a gully on the right and a short scramble takes you to the summit. It no doubt sounds complex, but it is very straightforward and a justly popular ascent, but one must descend the same way and it could be dangerous in the wet since the route is above very steep rocks.

Even if you don't climb to High Man you can still have a little thrill by scrambling on big holds to the top of Pisgah.

After a breather on top of Pillar and you have admired the views towards Gable, head to the south-west down a steep ridge to Wind Gap. There is a view across Wind Gap Cove to the prominent little summit of Steeple, towards which you must go next. Descend, then climb the rocky slope opposite, over tumbled rocks and then a grassy path, to more level ground and Scoat Fell, where a high wall vainly attempts to keep sheep away from the high crags. The scenery is marvellous and even more so if you continue westwards along the fell towards Haycock and follow the well-marked path out to the superb rocky little peak of Steeple, which you could see earlier. From there splendid views may be had across the dark depths of Mirk Cove back to Pillar and along the thickly forested miles of Ennerdale.

After retracing your steps to the wall on Scoat Fell, on the other side, beyond the many boulders scattered about, is a path heading south-westwards towards Red Pike, above the great combe of Mosedale. Having reached Red Pike,

descend the long and stony slope on a good path until it reaches the dip in the broad ridge, where Stirrup Crag rears up ahead.

A decision has to be made and walkers may often be seen dithering. You can climb up Stirrup Crag on a steep but good path and traverse Yewbarrow, which is a very good way, or you may follow the track down Overbeck to Bowderdale and walk back along the road, which is the dullest way to go.

The quickest and most sporting route to Mosedale used to be the descent of the screes from the depression in the ridge known as Dore Head. When there was some scree, it used to be great fun. But, like almost everywhere in the Lakes, there is none any more; it just lies in heaps at the bottom of the slope, leaving earth and rock, now partly grassed over. The slope itself is very steep and unrelenting. If time is of such importance that you must descend this way, then head well left of the direct line and, like a skier, find slanting zigzags down the grass and little ledges that will serve just as well, if not so quickly. You should arrive alive; if you tumble, it will be your own fault. Then you will be down on the green sward of Mosedale and can amble back to base alongside the beck.

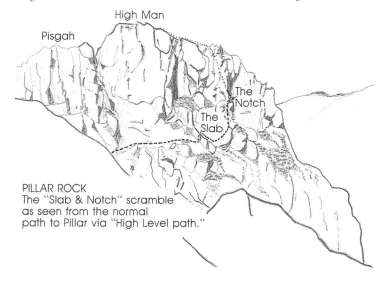

PILLAR ROCK
The "Slab & Notch" scramble
as seen from the normal
path to Pillar via "High Level path."

2. The Greater Mosedale Horseshoe: Yewbarrow, Red Pike, Pillar, Kirk Fell and Gable

Once you've seen Pillar Rock from the High Level Route you can look a little farther afield. My suggestion for a second marvellous walk is longer and more challenging, but the walk can be shortened by an escape at Black Sail Pass.

Park at Wasdale Head, or beside the head of the lake, or Overbeck, as you choose: you can't avoid half a mile of road at either end of the day. Whatever you do don't miss climbing Yewbarrow as the first stage. The steep grassy rib beyond a stile will get your heart and lungs going, but do persevere upwards rather than yield to the temptation to take a lower-level path that skirts under Yewbarrow.

Either scramble up the broad gully (where the path goes) or, more interestingly, keep going straight up the nose of Yewbarrow and you will be rewarded by enjoyable and easy scrambling on good rock up Bell Rib until you reach the summit ridge. You will pass a big cleft in the rocks called the 'Great Door' through which you may have a fine view of Pikes Crag and Scafell. As the view opens up there is the sight of a wonderful day ahead of you, starting along the rocky spine of Yewbarrow itself, which ends quite suddenly in the rocks of Stirrup Crag above Mosedale. The descent to Dore Head is short and easier than it threatens to be, but a steady uphill climb then follows to Red Pike.

Few people bother, but if you keep bearing left near the top up a little rocky bluff, you may find the stone 'armchair', carefully placed so that it looks out over Scoat Tarn. It is just off the main footpath, so that only those who seek will find it. Whether you miss or find this curiosity, the path traverses the summit ridge of Red Pike, where there are views down the combe at the head of Mosedale and of very impressive crags looming out of the depths. Unfortunately for the rock-climber, or even the scrambler, there is a lot of scree between the crags and the rock strata is not encouraging, so what rock routes are discovered are unlikely to remain popular for long.

Press on to Scoat Fell, and divert to Steeple to appreciate its fine situation and views, then on to Wind Gap and the stony slope beyond it to the summit of Pillar. Don't rush too fast, for you aren't half-way yet, but after peeping down to Pillar Rock from above, take the long and easy slope down the ridge north-east to the Black Sail Pass.

About fifty years ago I stood on this pass for the first time, loaded with a huge rucksack, and looked down with immense relief to the tiny speck of the Black Sail Youth Hostel at the foot of the Scarth Gap Pass. My friend and I were booked in for that night and we tottered downhill thankfully. When we arrived we found we had made a booking all right – for a month later; the tiny hostel was full. We shouldered our loads again and walked on despondently into the growing gloom and drizzle, down the long miles of the Ennerdale Forest. Rescue came at last when we saw the glint of light at the Forestry workers' cottages at Gillerthwaite and a most hospitable lady and her husband took the two waifs in, fed them and found them comfortable beds. The following morning the sun was shining again and we set off, but she would only accept a token payment after great pressure.

As you stand at the top of Black Sail Pass instead of descending to Ennerdale you should be scanning the hillside of Kirk Fell opposite. If your resolution is waning you may descend the Gatherstone Beck to get back to Wasdale, for this is your escape route. I hope that you won't need it, for you've come quite a way and it would be a pity not to do the rest.

It is not completely obvious how to get up and over Kirk Fell as you look at it from the Black Sail Pass, but up and over you must go to get to Great Gable. The side of Kirk Fell that you are looking at is not the shapely cone seen from beside Wastwater, rather a jumble of rocky buttresses and three scree-filled gullies. These, from a distance, offer some prospect of a way up but the stony 'path' towards them only reveals their nastiness in slimy detail. However, help is at hand for, if you cut back sharp right just before reaching the base of these gullies, a short rake slants easily on to the nose of the ridge above the steepest rock buttress. Here, surprisingly, is an iron fence post. Beyond it leads a very friendly little path, which spirals up small rock steps, passing more fence posts (or the sockets cut for them in the rock) to reach the top of the rise. When you reach what feels like it ought to be the summit, you'll find that it is actually half a mile away to the south and the continuing line of fence posts leads unerringly to it. From this, however, it is only a hop and a couple of skips over stony ground, passing the two halves of Kirk Fell Tarn (I suppose they were one entity once) then down the easy rocks of Rib End to reach Beck Head, the hause between Kirk Fell and Great Gable.

Right: The worn-out scree run down Dore Head.
Far right: The Scafells seen from the Great Door on Yewbarrow.

The final climb up the shoulder of Great Gable lies ahead and a steep path up scree beckons. However, beyond the scree, you'll probably need that surge of energy we can all summon when absolutely necessary, for the final scramble over those large, sharp-edged boulders that defend Great Gable's summit are rather tiresome. A rest here has been earned, believe me.

Finally, a path down the scree at the side of the rocks of White Napes leads to the grassy spur of Gavel Neese and towards the sun setting beyond Wastwater. That pint at the Wastwater Head Inn will never taste better.

3. Pillar via Looking Stead, Scoat Fell, Haycock and Seatallan

If you have done the last two walks you will not appreciate any repetition about going up to Black Sail via Gatherstone Beck and then up the track westwards to the top of Pillar, so I will say no more.

From Pillar descend to Wind Gap and then go up the rocky slope and the level grassy ridge beyond, to the walls on Scoat Fell. This time, after your visit to Steeple, don't head for Red Pike but continue along the side of the wall on the springy grass and, after a little descent, go up again to the gentle summit of Haycock. This is lonely country, softer in its contours and a little more off the beaten track. Just before reaching Haycock a path does descend steeply to the beginnings of the stream that becomes Nether Beck, which flows into Wastwater, and this is a useful escape route if you need it. My suggestion is that you stay on the broad ridge top, head south over the rocky ground of Gowder Crag and then stroll down open fell to the hause where a gentle climb leads to the sharpening ridge and the cairn on the summit of Seatallan. This must be one of the least-visited summits in the Lake District, consigned to being a lonely satellite of greater peaks, but visiting it enables you to avoid being constrained within the deep valley of the Nether Beck until you are ready to descend.

From Seatallan reverse the short ridge up which you came, or take a direct line south-east downhill to the hause at the head of the combe sheltering Greendale Tarn. Next pick your own line eastwards, down the rocky hillside, to join the Nether Beck and the footpath. On a fine summer's evening you'll find that there are some splendid pools, hidden away before you reach the road and Wastwater; these are just right for a cool dip.

3a. Alternative scramble to Pillar via Wistow Crags

A fine alternative to tramping up the shoulder of Pillar from Black Sail, and one which leads you very close to the summit, is this scrambling route up Wistow Crags in Mosedale; not on the uncomfortable crags of Red Pike but on the sunny south-facing slopes of Pillar.

Instead of going up to Black Sail, follow the track into Mosedale which descends from Wind Gap, then trend right as the slope steepens, cross the first stream-bed and make for the obvious two-tiered rock buttress on the right of the next scree gully. The left edge of the first tier overhangs the gully at one point. The lowest easy rocks just to the right of the main gully lead to a steep, blank wall or slab angled towards the gully. However, just to the right of this, an elegant rib of perfect rock with good holds leads upwards. The angle begins to ease and a series of ribs and little walls of superbly rough rock enable more height to be gained until more broken ground is reached after about three hundred feet. The line of the ridge curves a little to the right and then back left to the second tier of more compact rock, which is, however, easier than that lower down. It presents no difficulties, though the enjoyment is sustained. Scrambling fades into walking up the grassy neck connecting the buttress to the mountain and the walkers' path to Pillar is only a little farther up the last bit of the slope. Nearly a thousand feet in height is gained on a most enjoyable scramble of great merit in fine surroundings. It deserves to be better known.

3b. The main walk in reverse, with alternative scramble start on Middlefell

The slopes of Middlefell overlooking the point where the Nether Beck flows into Wastwater are agreeably craggy and even more attractive because they face south-east and consequently get plenty of sun – when there is any. The rock is thus clean and often dry, when that on the higher fells can be greasy and not very pleasant.

From Nether Beck bridge looking up the fell to its summit, there is an attractive buttress at a slightly lower level and to its right. This buttress gives the best part of the scrambling. Don't go tramping up the path alongside Nether Beck; instead walk up the steep fellside to the lowest rocks, where the scramble can be started just right of the scree gully. The more you keep to the left edge the more interesting is the scrambling. If you feel that this scramble is getting too hard, trend easily rightwards to find easier, but still excellent rock. This is particularly the case once you have crossed the terrace and reached the main crag, although the holds are good even when you are in the most exposed situations on the left-hand buttress. Once the steep bits are behind, there is still perfect rock, but at an easier angle and after a little walk to the left, you may get all the way to the summit.

The beauty of such a scramble is that it can give an interesting start to a day of uncertain weather prospects or when there is cloud on the high fells. Having reached the top of Middlefell you can make the gentle descent and steady climb up to Haycock and so on to Pillar and the rest of the round.

4. Pillar: routes from Ennerdale

Pillar Rock is accessible from Buttermere via the Scarth Gap as long as you can face two ascents and two descents. It is, however, a steep climb from the River Liza up through the forest to the foot of Pillar Rock and it is consequently unlikely ever to become a popular way.

Ennerdale is Forestry Commission territory and although, when I first started climbing on Pillar Rock, cars could be driven freely up the forest road, that facility is now under restriction. This tends to mean that, unless you have pre-planned carefully, the car will have to be left at the public car park near Bowness Knott, which is halfway along the north shore of the lake. Then it is a mile and a half before you get to the 'Nine Becks Walk' signpost and can shortly afterwards get across the River Liza. It is then still quite a long walk up Ennerdale before reaching the bottom of any of the good ridges heading up to Pillar from that side.

A traverse, which is, of course, not as popular as a round because of its transport problems, is nevertheless quite feasible and can be very enjoyable, from the west end of Ennerdale Water, along the lakeside and up one of the ridges from Ennerdale to Haycock and so on to Pillar.

On one very memorable occasion I planned to do just that, then to continue over the Scafells, but also to test the then-new wonder-fabric 'Goretex', which I had in the form of a bivouac-sac. My wife dropped me off at the end of Ennerdale Water in the early afternoon and I tramped steadily, with our two dogs and a far-too-heavy rucksack, alongside the south side of the lake and eventually got up Haycock and over to Pillar. It was very hot and sultry and thunderstorms started to develop as I descended the shoulder of Pillar to Black Sail. I decided not to climb over Kirk Fell but to follow the traversing path across its lower northern slopes, which leads to Beck Head. Then I picked up the Moses' Trod track, which leads under the great crags of the Ennerdale face of Great Gable.

Lightning was flashing as I settled down amongst the great boulders below Gable and I just managed to heat some food on my little stove before a torrent of rain put the flame out. I scrambled into my sleeping bag, which was inside the Goretex one, having put the dogs under a rocky shelter and covered it with a plastic dustbin liner. Of course, the dogs soon scratched the plastic to pieces, started to get wet and then wanted to join me in the bivouac-bag. The weather was so awful that I relented and allowed them in. Then I pulled the whole bag right over my head, closed it up like an envelope to keep out the pouring rain and wind, and managed to breathe comfortably and remain warm and dry, free from condensation, throughout the night. The dogs, naturally, were a dratted nuisance, wriggling and squirming around, so I doubt whether I slept for more than ten minutes at a time.

The following morning the rain had stopped but there was a thick mist which did not look as if it would disperse, I hadn't slept much and so the plan to go over the Scafells was abandoned. Anyway I tramped up to Windy Gap, down Aaron Slack to Styhead, up to Esk Hause and headed for Langdale. At about ten o'clock in the morning the mist began to clear and, as I tramped down Mickleden, Joss Naylor ran lightly past with a cheery wave and a word. I was glad to be rescued shortly afterwards from the Dungeon Ghyll car park by my wife. Joss was no doubt back in Wasdale before I got to the end of Mickleden.

None of the routes from Ennerdale to Pillar is very satisfactory for a good round, unless you take in the whole of Ennerdale – of which more later – or are prepared to face those five miles or so up or down Ennerdale. The best ridge is that which ends at Steeple, then you may go over to Pillar via Wind Gap and perhaps descend from the foot of the Rock back to Ennerdale. But, as the Irish might say, if I wanted to go up to Pillar, I wouldn't start from there.

Right: From the summit of Pillar across to the Scafell group.
Overleaf left: The west face of Pillar Rock.
Overleaf right: The head of Wastwater.

GREAT GABLE SECTION

1. Great Gable from Honister via Brandreth and Green Gable; return via Beck Head and Moses' Trod

This is a straightforward cigar-shaped walk without any complications and has the advantage, which many walkers find irresistible, of starting as high up the mountain as possible, on top of Honister Pass, where there is a good car park.

The most obvious way is to go westwards, grinding up the slope towards the quarries on Honister Crag. Then, when you realise that the track you are on is really heading for Haystacks, veer off it to the south, skirting Brandreth and so reach Gillercomb Head, just before the start of the climb up to Green Gable. If all you want to do is to get to Great Gable quickly this will be the fastest way. For a good walk, however, I suggest that you keep it for your return.

While you are at Honister and still full of energy, look farther left than the eroded way and set off up a less obvious track heading south-westwards, shadowing the line of the stream descending from Grey Knotts. Its rocky summit is a thousand feet above, but when you get there you will have the pleasure of treading fairly rough ground but be on the crest of the broad ridge running from Grey Knotts to Brandreth. There are fine views down into Gillercomb and to Borrowdale, as well as north-west to Grasmoor and High Stile. The slight descent from Brandreth brings you to a little tarn trapped in the rocks of the ridge and then a long, and at times stony, path leads up the slope to the top of Green Gable. This is a superb viewpoint, better than Great Gable, at least for the views down Ennerdale to Pillar and across Haystacks to Grasmoor and the Dale Head group. A short descent down the opposite slope and a zigzag scrabble up the other side leads to the summit of Great Gable.

Great Gable is unique in Lakeland for its memorial plaque, on the summit, commemorating those members of the Fell and Rock Climbing Club who died during the First World War but also because the plaque records a most remarkable gesture. This was the gift, by the Fell and Rock, of some 1,184 acres of Lakeland fell over 1,500 feet in height on both sides of the Styhead Pass, to the National Trust 'for the use and enjoyment of the people of our land for all time'. As Napes Needle on Gable saw the birth of rock-climbing, the Fell and Rock have adopted the Needle as the badge and symbol of the Club.

A hundred yards or so away from the summit and slightly lower is the Westmorland Cairn. Situated on top of the crags of the same name it affords a much better view of the patchwork of fields at Wasdale Head and also the length of Wastwater. Just below the crags is the narrow neck where the Napes ridges all converge: a useful spot to note mentally for further explorations on Great Gable.

To descend you should pick a way over the summit rocks towards the north-west shoulder of Great Gable and follow the cairned path steeply down towards Beck Head. The path continues up the slope beyond to Kirk Fell, but you should swing to the right, descend the fellside a little and find the narrow path running below the great crags of the Ennerdale face of Great Gable. This path leads immediately below the rocks, but lower down the slope is another path curving away from the crags and swinging round to the north in the direction of Honister and well below the summit of Green Gable. This lower path, named Moses' Trod after a smuggler who is reputed to have taken his packhorses that way to Wasdale, is the one that you want. It allows fast and easy going towards Brandreth where it connects with the main path near Grey Knotts before a straightforward return to Honister.

I once set out to do this walk in reverse, starting out along Moses' Trod. The weather, however, turned dramatically worse and I was soon in thick fog and pouring rain. Although I left it too late to take an accurate compass-bearing I felt certain that I knew where I was. It was quite a shock when, after passing below some steep rocks which looked strangely familiar, the all-too-certain shape of Napes Needle loomed out of the mist! I was 180 degrees wrong and on the wrong side of the mountain. I can only plead that I am as human as you – and what matters is to learn from the mistakes.

2. Great Gable from Seathwaite in Borrowdale

The road up Borrowdale forks at Seatoller, the main branch going over Honister to Buttermere and the other following the infant River Derwent to the little hamlet of Seathwaite, where it ends and there is parking space. The main footpath to Stockley Bridge and Styhead follows the valley bottom but my preferred route starts up Sourmilk Gill, whose foaming waters rush down the slopes of Base Brown directly opposite the farm. Go through the archway in the farm buildings on the right and cross the bridge spanning the beck beyond. The

High Stile, Haystacks and the Buttermere fells from Green Gable.

81

path ahead used to be one of the most eroded horrors in the Lakes District, but work in recent years has made climbing the rocky left bank of the gill a much pleasanter experience.

Once or twice the path edges through the trees very close to the line taken by the rushing beck, which can be quite a spectacular sight after heavy rain. Then, after a bit of a scrabble where the path wiggles up some slabs, you are above the trees and can go over a huge stile bridging a wall. By following the line of the stream you will soon enter the combe between Base Brown and Brandreth. Opposite is the rambling buttress of Gillercomb, of which more later; but for this walk bear left and tramp south-west up the steadily rising slope.

On a couple of occasions in winter, to give a more sporting variation to this part of the walk, I have chosen a line up the shoulder of Base Brown, via one or other of the broad gullies. I suspect these would not be so interesting in summer, for earth and scree, when banded together by frost and ice, can give quite a good footing, but they would not be so pleasant in warmer seasons. It doesn't matter whether or not you go below the slopes of Base Brown or over the top, for you still reach the neck which links Base Brown to Green Gable and may then press on steadily up the slope towards the latter.

I was once toiling up this slope on a hot summer's day when I came across two young men sitting amongst the boulders and looking very unhappy – with good reason. Somehow one had dislocated his knee. It had happened very suddenly and he had cried out to his friend as he fell over. His friend had turned to him, put his own foot down carelessly on the rough ground and had also fallen over, spraining his ankle. I was on my own at the time, but had to try something, so l helped the one with the dislocated knee to his feet so that he could use me as a crutch. We tottered a hundred yards or so when suddenly something clicked in the joint and he realised that he could walk again. So, we strapped up his friend's ankle and the pair of them stumbled off towards the safety of the valley.

From Green Gable descend to Windy Gap then climb the well-used track to the summit rocks of Great Gable, which can be such a busy place at lunchtime that you may find it more congenial nearer to the Westmorland Cairn. After lunch, there is a straightforward descent found by following cairns south-east from the summit towards Styhead Tarn. This path, the Breast Route, used to be very unpleasant, with many loose stones to skid on, but it had an expensive makeover a few years ago, thank goodness, and the effects of it have not all yet disappeared. Alternatively, you could consider reversing the descent to Windy Gap and then descend Aaron Slack, which is the natural groove going straight down towards Styhead Tarn. Like most direct routes, it is a steeper descent, but it can be more sheltered than the Breast Route and there is normally a stream running to provide a welcome drink on a hot summer's day.

Once Styhead Tarn is reached head back towards Borrowdale along the almost level Styhead Gill path. There is a half-mile or so of obvious bridle-way but, instead of staying with it, as soon as the trees are seen rising from the banks of Taylor Gill ahead, cross the beck to its left bank. A narrow path on the left side of the gorge soon allows a fine back view of the cascade, provides a pleasant traversing line through some trees and then slants down across fairly easy ground to reach the footbridge, the track under the archway and your transport.

2a. Alternative scramble in Sourmilk Gill

The waters of Sourmilk Gill pour down some very fine, open slabs at an amenable angle for scrambling and as long as you don't consider it seriously after very heavy rains – for the slabs disappear under the water – there is usually enough rock to give some pitches of pleasant scrambling. The path goes up the left-hand side of the gill, but it is better for scrambling to start up the right-hand side where a slab enables the first cascade to be overcome. Stay on the right-hand side to get past the next waterfall and the cascade pouring down a long groove. Above are some fine open slabs, which can be climbed for a long way until the angle begins to ease. The gill may then be left to join the path, but this will avoid the fine amphitheatre above, where the water shoots out from a square cut channel. Climb rock steps on the left-hand side, then a ledge leading back towards the waterfall brings a sudden arrival on to the open moor above. The roar and splash of the water among the trees is then all behind you and you can walk peacefully onwards into the combe.

2b. Alternative scramble on Gillercomb Crag

If you haven't spent too much of the day in Sourmilk Gill and are in the mood for another scramble to take you higher still, this is a golden opportunity not to

The patchwork fields of Wasdale seen from Needle Gully.

be missed. Above Sourmilk Gill you will emerge on to the soggy moor where Gillercomb Buttress is directly across the combe at its right-hand end. On the front of the buttress there are several classic climbs; the crag then bends round to reveal a very steep, upper wall which is separated from much easier-angled slabs on its right by a broad gully, below which are quite extensive screes.

The scrambler's route follows these easier slabs – once you have battled over the tiresome screes – which form the right wall of the gully. The rock is excellent, rough and solid, (though a bit greasy in the wet) and you can gain height comfortably up the slabby rib to a point where it steepens and traversing moves back left towards the gully seem advisable. Rather vegetated slabs above this point lead fairly steeply to the shoulder, where you can perch with the impressive upper wall to your left. The scramble continues up the edge of the upper crag and is easy until just near the top where two chimneys are reached, one above the other. Getting up these is really more rock-climbing than scrambling, but they can be easily avoided by simply traversing a bit farther rightwards away from the edge and so to the top. If this route is combined with the ascent of Sourmilk Gill, there is about 1,800 feet of scrambling, which must be one of the longest possible outings of its kind in the area. From the top of Gillercomb Crag it is of course a straightforward walk along the broad ridge top to join the path to Green Gable.

3. Great Gable by the 'Climbers' Traverse'
3a. Optional scrambles: 'Threading the Needle'; via Sphinx Ridge; on Westmorland Crags

Starting from Seathwaite in Borrowdale there is no problem in getting as far as Styhead Pass – just reverse the descent route via Styhead Gill described in the previous walk and continue past Styhead Tarn to the top of the pass.

If you are based in Wasdale the superb cone of Great Gable is seen at its very best, and you will also see the grassy spur descending straight towards you from the easy-looking rocks of the White Napes, with a footpath going straight up the line of the spur. This is Gavel Neese and the path, when you are bursting with energy and enthusiasm, is well nigh irresistible. I advise you to resist it nonetheless, for it is a lot farther than it looks and you are likely to be in a state of collapse by the time you reach the summit that way. In fact another footpath

branches off, traversing the fellside to Beck Head, which, although it may well have been part of the Wasdale side of Moses' Trod at one time, is now probably used more by walkers on Gavel Neese who realise that they have bitten off more than they can chew. So contain your impatience to get to grips with this fine mountain, ignore both of the above distractions and keep going east up the trade route to the top of the Styhead Pass.

If Wasdale was your starting point you must do an about turn, but if you have come from Borrowdale you must swing to the right to cross a plateau going gently upwards and westwards. In each case the objective is the unmistakable crag of Kern Knotts which comes into view ahead. This has a seventy-foot smooth wall facing you, split by two obvious cracks, the left hand one of which has a 'sentry box' in it and is the historic (and much-photographed) Kern Knotts Crack. The path scrabbles through the great boulders around the toe of Kern Knotts then gently continues upwards across rock and scree towards sharp ridges ahead. Just before crossing the great river of red scree that is Great Hell Gate a spring bubbles from below some smaller overhanging crags on the right, then, after crossing the scree, you are under the enormous impending crag of Tophet Wall. This is an impressive place but strictly the preserve of the rock-climber.

Leaving Tophet Wall behind, the path gets much closer to the steep rock and the Napes Ridges come into view. A little farther and the path forks. If you take the lower branch you will pass completely below the Napes and have a tiring scramble up the right-hand edge of the screes of Little Hell Gate to reach the top of the mountain. Stay with the higher track and look out for Napes Needle ahead and above, but remember that you will be seeing it from the other side and it will not be quite the view that you are probably expecting. Whichever way you go it will be scrambling rather than walking, but there are easier or slightly harder ways and the harder is just a variation on the easier in each case. I will attempt to describe them both as the occasions for the choice arise.

As you scramble up the bed of the gully below the Needle your first moment of decision arises, though in fact the classic, and well-scratched, way takes the harder route: 'threading the Needle'. For this, scramble up to the right of the base of the Needle then fight your way up the groove to the gap between the Needle and Needle Ridge. As you struggle into the cleft and look over you will realise that it was worth it, for there, ahead of you on the skyline, is the

Far left: Wasdale and the Sphinx Rock.
Left: Climbers on Napes Needle, Great Gable.

unmistakable black silhouette of the Sphinx Rock. The descent on the other side is easier and you can get down into the gully, then up the left hand side to a large ledge, well named the 'Dress Circle', for from there you get a good view of anybody climbing on the Needle. If you don't wish to 'thread the Needle', the same point can be reached by scrambling up the gully to the left of the Needle, instead of to its right. A rock path then leads leftwards below Eagle's Nest Ridge, down a few steps into a gully, then up again to pass behind a large flake of rock before descending into Eagle's Nest Gully. All the time you are traversing towards the Sphinx Rock and ledges below it are reached in a few more minutes.

The Climbers' Traverse really ends at the Sphinx Rock. You could scramble up to the gap between Sphinx and the steep buttress behind it, but there would then be a little rock pitch of ten feet or so to descend. It is also quite awkward reaching the gap if the rock is not dry. On the far side of the gap is Little Hell Gate but it is just a dreary trudge up endless scree to reach the top of the mountain. So stay on the Needle side of the Sphinx and go up the gully on its immediate right. As you climb it gets easier, bits of path appear and wind about and you will soon be at the narrow, grassy neck where all the Napes ridges converge. For a more sporting ascent to the same place (and a true scramble) leave the gully as soon as possible and tackle the rocky ridge itself on the left. Under good conditions this is an enjoyable alternative. Above, the broken rocks of Westmorland Crags block the way. The easier option follows the path detouring round to the left, grovelling up a nasty and loose slope, then go round to the right to reach the summit plateau.

The slightly harder, but much better way, from the top of the Napes Ridges, is to go horizontally rightwards on a faint path below Westmorland Crag, beyond the first little ridge to the second one then scramble up that, keeping to the right up a series of steps and avoiding going into the gully on the right if you can. Finally a short wall, behind a little pinnacle, leads to an airy finish and the Westmorland Cairn. It is much more satisfactory than the normal path.

The descent route will depend on whether you have to return to Wasdale or Borrowdale. For Wasdale, the best way is probably straight down Gavel Neese. Tripping lightly down scree and grass is as enjoyable going down (unless old age and decrepitude are catching up with you and your knees are nearly knackered) as it is purgatorial going up. However, if you must return to Borrowdale, the most interesting way is to go over the summit and descend to Windy Gap, climb up over

Green Gable and then go along the crest of the broad ridge of Base Brown. However, take care with the descent, for there are rock barriers not easily spotted from above. After grass and easy rocks, which form a sort of first step on the descent, the easy progress is suddenly halted by an upsurge of steep rocks and certainty gives way to dithering. A narrow path leads rightwards to a temptingly wide and vegetated gully cutting through the rim of crags, but ignore its apparent charms for its exit is very tricky, down a bare slab. It is better to cross the head of this gully, keeping well right, as if to descend to Seathwaite rather than into Gillercomb. You should then spot the path below. This is easily gained and then cuts back left, directly below the Hanging Stone, which waits poised to slip one of these days and obliterate some poor sheep or fell-walker unfortunate enough to be in its path. It is unlikely to happen before the next big earthquake. Once you are safely below and beyond it you may contour back towards Gillercomb at a convenient level to meet the path coming up from Sourmilk Gill and then descend safely back to the valley. In mist or bad weather, of course, it's better to avoid Base Brown altogether and take the signed path down Gillercomb itself.

4. The Ennerdale Horseshoe

This magnificent walk along the whole of the Ennerdale skyline is an experience that every fit Lakeland fell-walker should aim to do at least once. Twenty-one miles or thereabouts of continual up and down, over varied mountain terrain, will take the normal fit walker about twelve hours. Of course, it is a challenge which must be planned in advance, but to do it is to experience a walk of great beauty where the well-defined ridges are dramatically contrasted with the lowlands that edge the western sea.

By far the most preferable way to do the walk is clockwise from the western end of Ennerdale Water and it goes without saying that an early start is essential.

The first top to be visited is Great Borne. Our Victorian ancestors treated it with respect, as a grand viewpoint, which is probably why there is such a large cairn on its summit. I cannot quite recall precisely which route I took on my own first attempt, but there was a period when a local farmer was known to threaten walkers on his land with a shotgun. Maybe there is still a risk of that from his successors. Better to play safe and take the public footpaths from the big car park on the north shore of Ennerdale Water and head (irritatingly, in the wrong direction to begin

with) westwards for Flautern Tarn. Once the hause is reached, just before the descent to the tarn, you can safely turn south and uphill. From Great Borne, always excepting mist or bad weather, route-finding is straightforward – until the last few miles.

A narrow path runs lightly through heather over Starling Dodd and Little Dodd and then across the moor to the edge overlooking Buttermere to Red Pike. For the next section, if you've already walked the High Stile ridge, you will be on familiar ground again: marvellous views down to Bleaberry Tarn from High Stile, splendid vistas across to the Buttermere fells from High Crag, and those tantalising glimpses into the depths of Birkness (or Burtness) Combe. Then it is a knee-jarring descent down Gamlin End from High Crag to the Scarth Gap, a short climb up and over the delightful summit of Haystacks and a longer climb over what may be boggy stretches before the slope leads up to Brandreth. Not much more then to the head of Ennerdale: and once you've climbed over Green Gable and up those final slopes to the summit of Great Gable you will feel that you are, psychologically at least, at the half-way point.

I once set out when I was feeling reasonably fit, to do this round in twice Joss Naylor's record time of three and a half hours, that is, in seven hours. At Great Gable, after which I had decided I would be going downhill, I was on target: three hours and ten minutes. I had been running whenever I could, which is to say on all the downhill and on the level sections, and it had still taken me over three hours. How any human being could – in another twenty minutes – have done the whole circuit still has me baffled! In the event, by running the last three miles as hard as I could go, I managed it in two minutes outside my allotted time, but I was totally exhausted. I do not even remember my final descent route although I think that I may have descended Red Beck to the Ennerdale shoreline. To this day I do not know the precise route taken by the fell-runners.

In theory, after you've crossed Kirk Fell and reached Looking Stead, you could do the High Level Route to Pillar Rock, but in practice even the long trudge up to Pillar by the shoulder always seems tough. Comfort yourself with the thought that, after Pillar, it is generally downhill all the way, but in fact you've that rocky climb up to Black Crag out of Wind Gap and then, once you've reached Scoat Fell there's another little climb up to Haycock – and they all take their toll out of your dwindling reserves of strength. Fortunately you can't get lost along there even in a mist, for you follow an amazing stone wall for about five miles along the watershed.

After Haycock the contours become softer and the ground underfoot less rocky. With sufficient energy you could go fast along this section, but without it, it is more rewarding to go at a steady pace and watch the sun sinking low over the Irish Sea. On a later crack at this same walk, being older and slightly wiser and with far fewer 'hard man' pretensions, I sorted the last few miles out rather differently. As mentioned earlier, Haycock is a summit with two cairns, one on each side of the wall and it is this wall which now defines the route. It swings north shortly after leaving Haycock and is a completely reliable guide until it reaches the edge of a small Forestry plantation. This is crossed by making use of gates, tracks and stiles, which appear when needed, and the path then leads to the top of Crag Fell. The last actual top is Grike, which I had avoided on two previous attempts. However, this time I reached it and thankfully found a wire fence only fifty yards west of the top, which led directly towards the head of Ennerdale Water. It was shadowed by a faint footpath which, after a short but steep descent, soon led close by Crag Farm House and so back to the car park. Like me, you will have weary legs and tired feet on the completion of this walk, but you will also have wonderful memories of one of Britain's best mountain days.

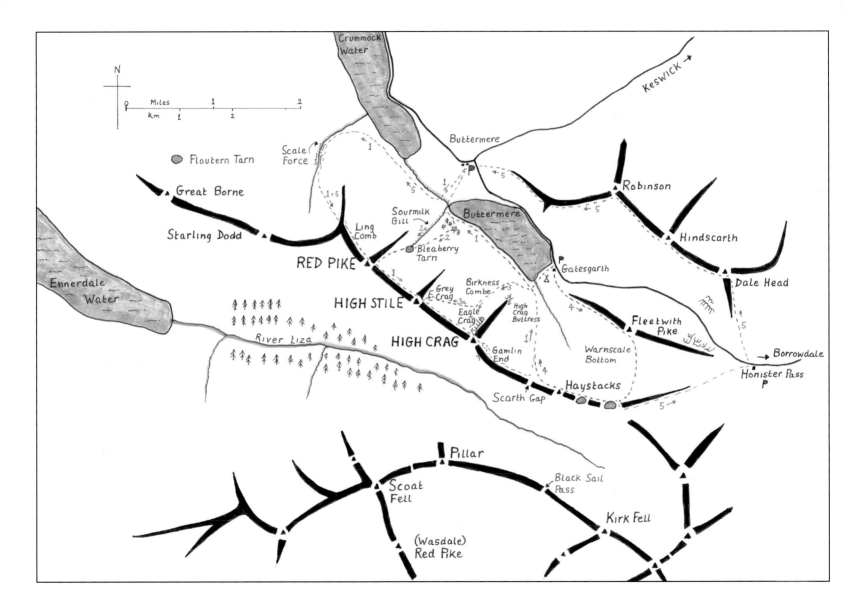

BUTTERMERE – THE HIGH STILE GROUP

	Approximate Time	Star Rating	Assessment of Difficulty
1. Scales Force, Red Pike, High Stile and High Crag Traverse	5 hours	***	—
2. Red Pike and High Stile via Birkness Wood and Bleaberry Tarn	4–5 hours	*	—
2a. Alternative start: scramble up Sourmilk Gill	add 1 hour	**	2
3. High Stile via Birkness Combe	4 hours	*	—
3a. Alternative scramble on Grey Crag in Birkness Combe	add 1/2–3/4 hour	**	3
4. Fleetwith Pike and Haystacks	4–5 hours	**	—
5. The Buttermere Round	7–8 hours	***	—

THE HIGH STILE GROUP

Three splendid combes are carved out of the north side of the ridge which separates the Buttermere valley from Ennerdale, and these form the perfect complement to the sparkling waters of Buttermere and Crummock Water which fill much of the valley. Scenically this is a most attractive area and delightful fell-walking country, with constantly changing views down the rocky cirques, across to the Grasmoor Group to the north and over to Pillar Rock and Gable to the south. The natural walking routes are up the combes, along their bounding edges and, of course, along their main connecting ridge. There are no attractive paths from the Ennerdale side of the main ridge, apart from the one over the Scarth Gap near the head of Ennerdale, so all the best walks start from the Buttermere side.

For reasons that are not very clear now, the hill on the northern end of the main ridge, Great Borne, was much favoured as a viewpoint in Victorian times. However, the approach path from either Ennerdale Water or Crummock Water via Flautern Tarn must be one of the boggiest in the entire Lake District, and

although Great Borne is the first peak on the main ridge it is now rarely visited except as the normal start to the great Ennerdale Round. The Ennerdale Round was dealt with in the chapter on Pillar so now let's make a start on what is the longest and probably the best walk traversing the High Stile ridge.

1. Scales Force, Red Pike, High Stile and High Crag Traverse

There is plenty of parking near the inns in Buttermere village and then fenced lanes – which after a prolonged wet spell can themselves be nearly as bad as the bogs near Flautern Tarn – lead across the strip of flat land between Crummock Water and Buttermere. A consolation in autumn is that there are many mature blackthorn bushes, which you can note for the return journey, as home-made sloe gin is a marvellous cockle-warmer around Christmas time.

Once across the flat land the path skirts alders to the north-west, then you must hop and step from stone to stone to avoid muddy patches before veering to the left following the general direction of Scale Beck, which is rushing out of Ling Comb high above. In its dash for Crummock Water it makes a huge leap in a slender waterfall, Scales Force, which eventually becomes evident through the trees choking the gorge. Scrabble steeply up the path on the left-hand side of the waterfall and then, still steeply, follow a series of trenches eroded in the heather, which continue uphill but now at right-angles to the line of the stream.

Soon you will emerge on the open plateau above and can then walk over to the rim of rocks encircling Ling Comb. Ahead and across the cirque the dominating shape of Red Pike rears up, and it is soon clear why this one is a genuine Red Pike because exposed earth on its eroded flanks is distinctly red in colour. The view from Red Pike is good, but it is even better once you have descended a little to the rim of Bleaberry Combe, followed the path round it and continued up to High Stile.

Bleaberry Tarn sparkles below frowning crags and the views back across the combe towards Crummock Water, Mellbreak and Loweswater are exhilarating. I get so lyrical over this view that I once described it in detail to a party of carpet trade colleagues who were strangers to the Lakes, but who had been cajoled by me into going there for a 'little walk' one cold March day. I had to describe it in detail, for we were in thick mist and there was almost nothing to be seen at all. Years later they were still pulling my leg about it.

From the summit of High Stile the path contours round the rim of the mighty Birkness Combe (sometimes spelt Burtness), which is flanked in the sunshine by Grey Crags below and in the shadows by the awe-inspiring Eagle Crag, which soars steeply from the depths far below. There is then a short climb up to the summit of High Crag and a welcome opportunity for a breather.

Nowadays the descent which follows, on grass and shale, down Gamlin End, has been greatly helped by the creation of man-made steps in judicious places to counteract erosion. Modern fell-walkers are being pampered, for it was not always thus. As with Dore Head (mentioned above in the chapter on Pillar) there used to be a lot of scree on this slope and I well recall exhilarating descents, taking huge sliding strides down it. Oh dear! I must myself have been one of those whose actions caused all those little stones to end up at the bottom of the slope. We never even thought about it, just revelled in the sense of speed under control on such shifting ground. It did need a certain panache and skill to do properly; some found the knack quickly, but others were not so lucky.

One of this latter kind of scree-runner was in the jolly party of work colleagues whose luck ran out when he followed my advice about 'running' all too literally. As I was familiar with the slope and it was misty, I had first explained what to do and then demonstrated it, showing the line of descent to take, stopping as I reached the first place where the angle relented. I turned to call to my friend to follow, but was flabbergasted to see him already launched and running, nay sprinting, in great leaps and bounds towards me, with no braking action at all and totally out of control. I watched, horror-struck and powerless, as he hurtled past me at great speed and then inevitably crashed into the fellside. He was wearing an anorak I had lent to him and although he said he was miraculously uninjured the rips in the garment told their own story. He drank an awful lot of my whisky that night, which I always suspected was to anaesthetise the pain of the bruises.

At the bottom of Gamlin End the path is almost level for a short way, then it undulates over some little outcrops of rock before a steeper descent, once more down an improved path, to reach the track that crosses Scarth Gap. It is then a straightforward path, although sometimes leg-jarringly rocky and uneven, that takes you downhill towards Gatesgarth Farm.

Walking down this same path recently, in mid-May, I was astonished and delighted to see a huge area of wild bluebells stretching towards Haystacks and carpeting the open fellside. It was a wonderful sight that I felt privileged to have seen.

To complete the circuit, all that is needed is a pleasant ramble back to Buttermere village along the lake's southern shore. If it is autumn and you have time, don't forget those plump and juicy black sloes.

For the record, there is another way of ascending to, or descending from, High Crag, although when I tried it there were few signs of usage. It is perhaps best described in ascent. Take the path from Gatesgarth to Birkness Combe then, after passing over the mossy lip at its entrance, climb the grassy slope beyond and trending leftwards directly towards High Crag Buttress (which is the largest lump of vertical rock in sight). You will reach an obvious rock-littered rake slanting just to the right of the buttress. Clambering up this in turn leads almost directly to the top of what has been called 'Sheepbone Rake' (by Alfred Wainwright, I believe) but it looked to me like a very wide, steep, rubble strewn and very unattractive

gully heading from bottom right to top left. Anyway, that is now below you and it needs only a brief scramble up broken ground to reach the north top of High Crag; this affords extensive views over Buttermere. Just a little higher and you are on the main top where you join the ridge path and the normal descent route down Gamlin End.

2. Red Pike and High Stile via Birkness Wood and Bleaberry Tarn

This walk is short and sharp and uses the most direct of the recognised paths to Red Pike. If you are coming after a wet spell of weather you may have to squelch and slop along those muddy lanes again from Buttermere village, but this time take the more southerly-heading one to reach the other side of the flat land near the bottom of Sourmilk Gill. This pours in a foaming cascade from Bleaberry Tarn high above and forms a very obvious feature of the fellside when seen from the Newlands Hause road.

Leaving the lakeside path, follow the other one rising into a belt of larches and pines. Although this causes some sneaking doubts, as it initially strikes uphill diagonally away from your desired direction, it soon swings back right and steeply upwards. The only slight drawback to this path is that the risers on the made rock steps are sometimes uncomfortably high. (Should you ever descend by this route you will know what I mean: in places you practically leave one leg stuck up behind you, with the foot at waist level, so that you lurch downhill with a great tendency to topple over. Going uphill, thankfully, seems easier.) Having gained useful height, this path crosses the stream emerging from Bleaberry Tarn and feeding Sourmilk Gill; the Tarn itself is just ahead. The last part of the ascent is then something of a trudge up the rather worn flank of The Saddle until you are actually on it, with a final pull to the summit of Red Pike. You may then either continue over to High Stile to reach Scarth Gap and then return, or take the opposite direction along the main ridge to return via Scales Force.

A different and much more interesting way misses out Red Pike but goes more directly to High Stile and is not marked on any map. Head for Bleaberry Tarn as before but then swing south (left) instead of north, and climb up on to the bilberry-covered ledges of the rocky ridge that separates High Stile from Birkness Combe. You will be on virtually untrodden ground, and if it's late August or September and you go slowly enough to see them, you may enjoy juicy bilberries

where most people never think of going. I lost a pair of sunglasses up there years ago but I don't suppose I'll ever get them back.

2a. Alternative start: scramble up Sourmilk Gill

Much of the water from Bleaberry Tarn foams down great sweeps of slabs which lie at an easy angle in the lower half of this gill and which provide the line of the route. The path crosses the bottom of the gill and you then head upwards, negotiating a lot of boulder debris before reaching the clean slabs. Keep on the rocks where they can be most easily climbed – that is, usually as close as possible to the rushing waters, without actually joining them in their headlong dash for Buttermere. In fact there are no particular difficulties in the lower section and it is most enjoyable.

The upper part of the gill is more constricted and with fine scenery; but occasional excursions on to either bank may seem necessary, depending on the amount of water in the gill and your willingness to take a ducking. It always seems to me to be an unusually long scramble, but it is most entertaining and ends quite suddenly, just below the outflow from Bleaberry Tarn. It should give no problems to moderately experienced exponents of this art, or to active fell-walkers with a taste for adventure. It is certainly a much more interesting way of getting up to the Tarn than the normal trudge and an exhilarating approach to a fine ridge.

3. High Stile via Birkness Combe

Normally the way up the middle of Lakeland combes, as opposed to their retaining ridges, are not so interesting; but Birkness Combe is rather special because it is high and lonely. A lovely clear stream tinkles down from far up it, and it has the great and impressive Eagle Crag brooding in shadow at its head. For a taste of grandeur and what Wordsworth might call 'sublimity', it is certainly worth a tramp up to the main ridge this way.

From Gatesgarth Farm at the foot of Honister, head off as for the Scarth Gap, but as soon as you cross the last stream flowing towards Buttermere lake from Warnscale Bottom turn right instead of left. A slanting track then heads upwards at a convenient angle under a rock buttress with a commemorative plaque to some lads who sadly died when they were practising abseiling from a great rock which inexplicably collapsed. Then pass over a mossy lip and climb steadily up into the combe itself.

One morning, on the lower part of the splendid climb of 'Eagle Front', which I was doing with the Lakeland artist Jill Aldersley, we became aware of a most marvellous aerial drama taking place. Without warning a peregrine falcon suddenly launched an attack on a pigeon and because we were ourselves quite high up, the action took place almost on our level. We were absolutely fascinated as we saw the falcon, then a fairly rare bird in the Lake District, and which must have been perched high on our crag, swoop in a long shallow dive towards the pigeon, which was clearly unaware of the impending attack. The dive seemed to last seconds, and then there was a puff of white and a thud as the falcon struck and a burst of white feathers flew. We thought that it was all over for the pigeon, but somehow the peregrine had mistimed its attack. Both birds tumbled in the air, but the pigeon recovered first and then flew like the wind, weaving and twisting as it fled for its life down the combe towards the lake. The falcon, although it chased its prey and looked for a moment as though it might yet succeed, was no match for the pigeon's speed and so it escaped, minus a few feathers. It had all happened in silence, apart from the report at the moment of impact, but as the falcon turned and headed back towards its eyrie on Eagle Crag and we heaved sighs of relief for the pigeon, the air was rent by three screaming cries from the thwarted predator.

As the path peters out high in the combe there is an escape by keeping close to the right side of Eagle Crag and then scrabbling up a grotty, but negotiable gully. It is the rock-climbers' descent route and leads to the main ridge above, where the path threads through boulders and you can head in either direction.

3a. Alternative scramble on Grey Crag in Birkness Combe
Instead of scrambling up the edge of Eagle Crag to climb out of Birkness Combe, a more attractive way – which is also usually in the sunshine – is to pick a way up the three main rock tiers that go to make up Grey Crags. In fact, this way combines several Moderate rock-climbs into one longer expedition and some rock-climbing experience is desirable. The climbing standard is mostly Easy, though, and as long as it is not attempted unroped in the wet, because the rock can be greasy in those conditions, this is an entertaining way up.

The lowest of the buttresses is Harrow Buttress and the route goes up it. A traverse by a ledge on the right of the lowest rocks leads to a deep chimney, a leftward escape to a good groove and then another escape left to avoid an overhang. Easier rocks then lead to the ridge at the top of the buttress, with a gully on the right. Across this is Chockstone Ridge which forms the next section. It is climbed in steps directly, or bypassed to the left at the top, depending on your own confidence. The final section is another buttress, but it is broken into large towers which are partly separated from the mountain. If you can't find an easy climb into the obvious recess go round to the left and then go up the gully on the right at the back. Within seconds you are landed happily on the main ridge.

4. Fleetwith Pike and Haystacks
Haystacks is the rocky wall, seamed by several dramatic, but crumbling and dangerous gullies, that forms a cirque round Warnscale Bottom and its traverse is both popular and enjoyable. Many people doing this walk start from Honister Hause, because of the height gained by parking at the top of the pass rather than at the bottom. But if you do start from Honister you are obliged to tramp up the very worn track past the relics of the former Drum House (for the old slate-workings on Fleetwith Pike), and then towards Haystacks, past a rather strange climbing hut half-buried in the old slate tips.

Although if you start through the old slate quarry you will save yourself a bit of effort climbing uphill, you will also deny yourself the pleasure of a much more attractive round trip involving a traverse of Haystacks. A better way is to go from Gatesgarth Farm at the bottom of Honister, and almost immediately start to climb the north-west ridge of Fleetwith Pike. Do not allow a memorial cross on the ridge to cast too much gloom or foreboding on your soul, for the ridge is well-defined and has a good path all the way up its crest, and you can watch the toy motorcars in the pass below hooting and barging their way up and down.

It is straightforward uphill walking but the view down the Buttermere valley, which is dramatic from the top of Honister, is better still from up there. After a while you are high above Honister Crag and the road below is lost to view. Avoid quarry workings on the summit and head south-east in an arc to pick up the track that comes from Honister past the climbing hut and drops

down the pony track into Warnscale Bottom. Don't, of course, descend, but head south-west across the boggy bit below the slate spoil-heaps and round the rocky rim above Green Crag. It is then gently upwards over and around rocky eminences and heathery lumps where little tarns sparkle. Blackbeck Tarn and Innominate Tarn are like jewels in their settings, and you may often have fine views towards Great Gable and Kirk Fell on this stretch.

The highest point on Haystacks is a bare rocky height with a tiny tarn immediately below it. From here, High Crag and Gamlin End are visible immediately across the Scarth Gap below, which is, of course, the next objective.

In earlier years I treated this descent to the Scarth Gap rather cavalierly. In fact it is a descent which deserves some respect, for it is not immediately obvious and when it becomes so it can still be a little intimidating. The reason is that it proceeds down a series of either rock steps or grooves, some of which are rather steep. There is little real risk, but it is the apparent difficulty which seems to make some walkers' knees turn to jelly. Watch for three more old iron fence posts of the same kind as the one you will notice embedded in the rock on the summit: they indicate a good line of descent. After the fourth one stone cairns lead leftwards to the foot of a gully and you are then below the defences. The way back to Gatesgarth is then obvious down the track and you will not have to retrace any of your steps or trudge up the Honister road to regain your transport.

5. The Buttermere Round

This is one of those classic walks which really must be on the list of every active fell-walker who is willing to accept the challenge of an energetic day on the fells. Having done it six or seven times in both directions, I can say without hesitation that the best way to do it is anti-clockwise. First go from Buttermere to Scales Force then traverse the High Stile–High Crag ridge. As previously mentioned, the descent of Gamlin End is much pleasanter than going upwards in the opposite direction and by the time you have traversed Haystacks and reached the top of Honister you have actually done more than half the distance. This is a natural place for a short rest before the taste of purgatory you will probably then experience in the trudge up to Dale Head that follows.

I did this walk several times in the company of one particular friend with whom I always had a bit of what I might describe as 'uphill rivalry'. On a boring stretch of walking such as this one up to Dale Head we both knew that such sections were best got over as quickly as possible. Consequently we surreptitiously started to walk uphill just a little faster than we might otherwise have done. We cut little corners. We didn't pause at all in places where we would both dearly have loved to stop. We even caught each other (but only out of the corners of our eyes of course!) doing little runs and spurts when we thought the other wasn't looking. Finally, all subterfuge thrown to the winds, we panted uphill as fast as we could go, pulses hammering and sweat running into our eyes, each absolutely determined that the one would not get to the top before the other! As you may imagine, we usually arrived in a state of collapse. He passed away some years ago and I still miss him.

A swig from the water bottle, a rest, a look at that splendid view down the Newlands Valley and the knowledge that it is more or less downhill all the way, do wonders in reviving the weary flesh. It is not over yet, of course, but what remains is mostly pleasant tramping and even the boggy horrors of Buttermere Moss, after you have left the summit of Robinson, can be more easily avoided when you are approaching them from above. The final stretch down those well-made grassy zigzags to the Sail Beck and Buttermere village are thankfully straightforward and you are soon down, glowing with the pleasure and satisfaction of having done one of the finest of Lakeland's walks.

Great Gable from Haystacks with Innominate Tarn.

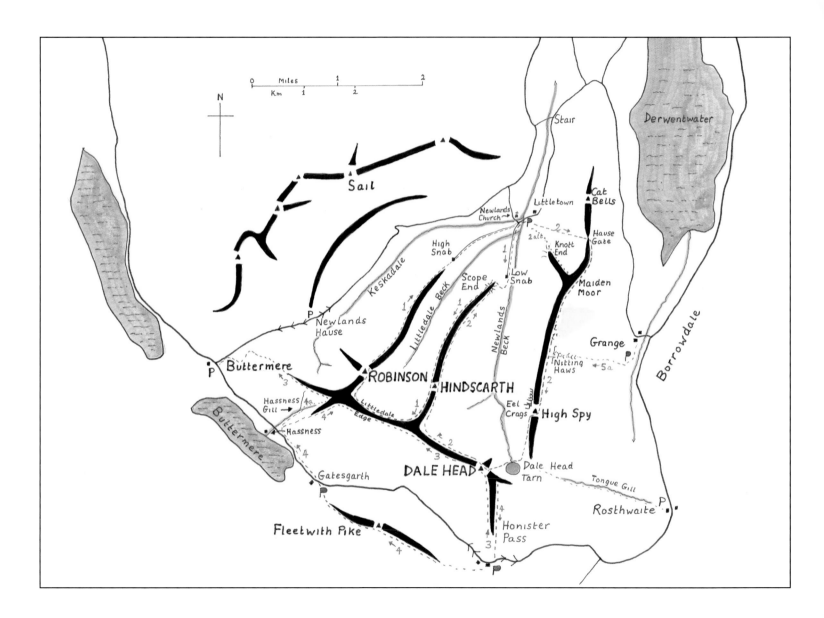

DALE HEAD GROUP – THE DERWENT FELLS

	Approximate Time	Star Rating	Assessment of Difficulty
1. Hindscarth and Robinson from Newlands	4 hours	**	—
2. The Newlands Round: Maiden Moor, High Spy, Dale Head and Hindscarth	4–6 hours	***	—
3. Traverse of the main ridge from top of Honister to Buttermere village	3–4 hours	—	—
4. Hassness to Robinson, Dale Head and Honister; descent by the north-west ridge of Fleetwith Pike	4–5 hours	*	—
4a. Alternative scrambling start via Hassness Gill	5 hours	*	2
5a. The Dalehead Group from Borrowdale: scramble up Nitting Haws to High Spy Ridge	2–3 hours	—	1–2

DALE HEAD GROUP: THE DERWENT FELLS

1. Hindscarth and Robinson from Newlands

The three ridges of this group are like the three prongs of a fork without a handle, pointing towards Keswick. The finest is probably the central one, from Scope End up to Hindscarth, because it is the sort of ridge that children of all ages enjoy best of all; the way goes tripping round and over little rocky bluffs through heather and over grass, always with another little surprise just around the corner.

Park for this route near the hump-backed Chapel Bridge, which is just beyond Littletown Farm (with a tree in its yard whose dead boughs seem frozen in a demented grimace). Having crossed the bridge, turn left just by the tiny and delightful Newlands Church and follow the track to Low Snab Farm, which is at the foot of Scope End.

There are some obvious mining spoil-heaps on the hillside just behind the farm. Once through the last gate, turn right on to the fell and you will pass the mine workings of the old Goldscope Mine, abandoned a century or so ago. Press on up the end of the spur to reach its crest.

Once there, the walking is a delight. There are fine views ahead to the end of the ridge of Robinson, and particularly over to Sail and the rest of the Buttermere fells. There are a couple of places where the path goes either up rocks, in an easy scramble for young children, or round them for parents – and the interest is well maintained until the last pull up to the summit when it is more open and a little steeper. My young son, who had cheerfully rushed up everything lower down, insisted that Dad carried him on his back up this bit! Fortunately the large cairn that is seen at the top of the final rise, although not the summit, is well-built and hollowed out to form a splendid shelter from the wind. It is an ideal spot for lunch and if it is at all windy, don't despise this opportunity, for there isn't much other shelter to be found on these rounded fells.

Walk on now, past the actual summit cairn, to join the line of the main watershed at Littledale Edge. Obviously one could turn left and go over to Dale Head, but leave that for another, longer day. Turn right and after a slight descent climb back up alongside the fence and so round to the summit rocks on Robinson. There are fine views down to Buttermere and Crummock Water and the Honister Pass a long way below. Even if the weather turns hostile it is best to stick to the planned walk so don't be tempted to escape down Littledale, instead of traversing Robinson. It is very wet and tussocky and there is no real path down there until you get to the point where the beck tumbles over some fine waterfalls, and that is a long way down. It is better to complete the descent down the end of Robinson, where the path runs alongside the edge of quite striking crags. It is well used and after a little 'bad step' at the shoulder (on Blea Crag) where there is a rocky bit to negotiate, it joins the straight and narrow, but grassy, ridge (High Snab Bank) that runs down parallel to your route of ascent earlier in the day.

I'll never forget descending this ridge from Robinson one February day when there was a lot of new, and very wet, snow on the fells. I had my two cocker spaniels with me at the time – marvellous dogs, but quite heavy – and the snow balled up on their fur. This happened especially between their legs, so that they became more and more bandy. However much I tried, I could not remove it fast enough. By the time we were on the descent the problem had become so severe that neither of them could walk at all. I was feeling pretty exhausted myself by then, but I had no choice but to shove one of them in my rucksack and carry the other over my shoulders. I tottered down to Low High Snab at the end of the ridge, with melt-water running down my neck, and joined the metalled road which runs back to Newlands church. With great relief I emptied a pint or so of water from the inside of my rucksack and was I glad to get off the fells that day.

2. The Newlands Round: Maiden Moor, High Spy, Dale Head and Hindscarth

One may start this excellent circuit of the heights above the Newlands valley by going up Scope End first, but, since we've already been that way on the last walk, how about a change and this time use the Hindscarth to Scope End ridge as the way of descent?

The start is again from Littletown – with that demented tree again – but this time a bridle-track heads east under the rocky humps of Knott End. Following this soon leads to the main ridge at Hause Gate, with the attractive little summit of Catbells along the ridge to the north. There's a fine view from the hause, but it is better a little farther on, once the cairn on Maiden Moor is reached.

May I, however, suggest another but more direct way to reach the heights; start by walking up the bridle-track towards Hause Gate, but turn off it almost

immediately. Climb south-east, directly up the spur connecting Looking Crag with Knott End and High Crags. This leads to Bull Crag and the cairn on Maiden Moor. It is hardly a scramble, for no scrambling is actually necessary at all, but you can zigzag about a bit if you like and climb up the best bits of rock. It is a steeper but quieter and rarely trodden alternative.

Derwentwater with its islets, the tree-covered crags of Borrowdale and all the sylvan beauties of the Vale of Keswick lie below. One may not quite agree with Dr Brown, of Cambridge, who, writing about 1750, stated that the 'full perfection of Keswick consists of . . . Beauty, Horror and Immensity united'. We live in a more prosaic age, but we can agree that you can get a good sight of it from this vantage point. I recall once standing on the dome of St Peter's in Rome and hearing a little old lady say to her companion, 'Eee Aggie! we're closer to 'Eaven than t'Pope is up 'ere!' Nowadays adjectives such as 'nice' are more likely to spring to mind than 'sublime'. More's the pity, because it is undoubtedly the power of human emotion that transforms our landscape, wherever it may be, and this is a splendid view of its kind. I still prefer the view in the other direction, across the ridges of Scope End and Robinson rather than that towards Keswick.

Over the next couple of miles the well-marked path traverses the broad back of the ridge, narrowing as it climbs a little to the cairn on High Spy. There you are above the rocks of Eel Crags (not to be confused with those on the Buttermere fells) falling away to the Newlands Beck. Eel Crags do have some rock-climbing on their isolated buttresses, but it is not easy to gain access to them, as they are not only surrounded by scree but are also buried in vegetation. My own recent visits (in the twenty-first century), have felt very like those that the pioneers must have experienced at least sixty years ago. Such crags are not currently in favour. Nowadays climbers can easily fly off to Spain, Sardinia or Greece for sunshine routes on seaside crags; how long will the cheap flights continue?

From High Spy there is a good view over to Dale Head and its crags, but one must then descend quite a way to reach Dale Head Tarn. This lies on the hause where the valley path from Newlands meets one from Borrowdale and also one from Honister. The climb that is to follow used to be quite a struggle, up a steep slope that was alternately rocky or loose shale, close to and then on the edge overlooking the Newlands valley. It was hardly a path, more a scar. Nowadays there is a man-made rock staircase, especially up the shaly parts, which makes it a

pleasanter ascent. However, there is still the same sense of achievement once you reach the cairn on the summit rocks of Dale Head and the view back to Eel Crags can be particularly striking.

There's nothing so tough on the rest of the walk, for your height has already been gained and little is lost on the traverse of Hindscarth Edge towards the hause between Hindscarth and Dale Head. Another climb follows, but it is a short one, curving out towards Hindscarth itself. With the wind in your hair, a firm path under your boots (or trainers, for this is also excellent fell-running country) and fine views you can hardly fail to enjoy yourself. Once the summit is reached there follows the descent of a shaly part near the top, but that will soon be over. Eventually you will be able to revel in the delights of the fine ridge all the way down Scope End to Low Snab.

3. Traverse of the main ridge from the top of Honister to Buttermere village

For fell-walkers with wheels it is a well-nigh irresistible temptation to get as high as possible up any road before starting a walk, and in this case it is probably the best way. There is a large car park at the top of Honister Pass beside the Youth Hostel and the adjacent slate-workings; you can either leave the car in the hope of thumbing a lift back up the Pass later on, or leave it in the capable hands of your long-suffering partner who will hopefully return with it to the village.

Cross the road and walk up a grassy slope going due north, on a well-marked path, for a good half hour's uphill trudge towards Dale Head. Don't expect this to be enjoyable, apart from the satisfaction of getting your physical engine going properly with the exercise, for the views are negligible. However, quite suddenly there is the well-made cairn on the top of Dale Head and the breath-taking view down the Newlands Valley all the way to Skiddaw. Crags fall away steeply at your feet and three fine ridges, all just asking to be walked, stretch away in front of your gaze.

Walk easily north-west along the broad ridge towards Hindscarth, on a good path with occasional rocky sections and stretches of springy peat and grass. It is an easy diversion out to Hindscarth summit, because the main path does just that, but in misty conditions it is advisable to watch your compass, for you may gently veer along what seems to be the main ridge and descend into the wrong valley without realising it. Beyond the point where the Hindscarth ridge meets the main one there

is a short descent and then another climb up towards Robinson's summit, which is simply the highest pile of rocks in sight.

While heading towards Buttermere village the line of the descent should be clear down a fairly steep path towards Buttermere Moss. With the advantage of height it should be possible to pick out a way over relatively dry ground to avoid getting wet feet while crossing the boggy wilderness.

The soggy path does, however, eventually lead to a nicely graded zigzag descent track which, although now eroded away in places, must obviously at one time have been very suitable for ponies. It leads pleasantly down to the Newlands Hause road just a little way out of Buttermere village.

4. Hassness to Robinson, Dale Head and Honister; descent via the north-west ridge of Fleetwith Pike

This is one of the less obvious but very enjoyable possibilities that will appeal, particularly to walkers who already have some experience of these fells.

Hassness is the striking white house amidst beautiful trees on the north shore of Buttermere lake, near to where the waters of Hassness Gill pour down from the fellside above. In summer, because of the trees in the vicinity, it is difficult to see that there is a fine, steep, but mostly grassy spur which forms the right bank of Hassness Gill. In winter it is more obvious when the leaves are off the trees, but seen from the High Stile ridge on the other side of Buttermere the spur is obvious enough and is the line of ascent.

When staying at Hassness or Birkness there should be no parking problems, but one may always park near Gatesgarth Farm and walk down the road, before heading upwards on the path up Hassness Gill. (It is interesting to note that the farm has now installed its own pay-as-you-park ticket machine. It has already welcomed campers for years but in these days after the great foot-and-mouth fiasco of 2001 the tourist pound is even more important to the farm economy. It remains a scandal that the government of the day did its best to destroy the outdoor leisure industry, as well as millions of animals, supposedly to protect agricultural exports.)

After a little way the path leaves the stream by a stile and climbs the grassy spur, following the fence. This is steep but the angle eases eventually and then leads to the main ridge, with the summit of Robinson only a hundred paces away. The walking is easier and you can stride out on a good path along Littledale

Left: On the Scope End to Hindscarth ridge; Robinson on the right.
Overleaf left: On the final slope to the top of Hindscarth; Grasmoor group in the background.
Overleaf right: To Crag Hill and Wanlope from Robinson's summit.

Edge towards Hindscarth, and then along Hindscarth Edge to Dale Head. Suddenly the pains of the long trudge up from Honister become the pleasures of a fast and easy descent. Don't go down too fast, though, as you'll need a few springs left in your knees for the next section.

There is nowadays much more activity at the slate-work buildings at Honister Pass than there has been for many years and even organised sight-seeing trips into the old mine levels. For fell-walkers the bonus is that the previously badly eroded path heading west and uphill from the pass has been much improved in its lower part. As the angle eases it continues across peaty ground, with occasional visible remains of the old slate-hopper railway, heading for the old Dubs Quarry (or Haystacks). One could, of course, continue along this route and follow the footpath down the line of waterfalls along Warnscale Beck and so get down to Gatesgarth. However, you would then miss out more interesting walking than you would gain and it is better to turn off the main track to the right (before an obvious path branches left towards Brandreth and the Gables) and go instead up and along the edge of Honister Crag, and on to the summit of Fleetwith Pike. This is a good viewpoint for virtually the whole length of Buttermere and Crummock. Then, when you are ready to descend, the fine little ridge of Fleetwith Edge takes you down a good path north-westwards back to Gatesgarth.

4a. Alternative scrambling start via Hassness Gill

Instead of following the path, as it breaks away to go up the grassy spur on the right side of Hassness Gill, you may continue up the line of the stream and so enter the main ravine. Potter up the watercourse to a little reservoir where the stream divides. It is a toss-up which way to go next but the left branch of the beck goes up a little gorge and looks more inviting. If, however, there is a great deal of water pouring down the beck, a scramble up the buttress on the right could be a better way. You reach – as you nearly always seem to do – a little amphitheatre into which three streams pour and probably the best way is to the left, where the water runs over slabs. These provide an enjoyable way up and, eventually, out. If there is too much water to use the slabs in the stream you can instead still scramble for a while up the broken rocks just to the right. Once you have emerged on to the open fellside a right-trending line to the east will soon lead up to Robinson's summit and to the rest of the walk.

5. The Dalehead group from Borrowdale: scamble up Nitting Haws to High Spy Ridge

Sadly, in my view there is no good horseshoe walk to be done on these fells from Borrowdale. The path from Rosthwaite, which simply strikes up the broad ravine of Tongue Gill to the disused quarries of Rigghead and then by slag-heaps to the hause where Dale Head Tarn is to be found, has little to recommend it. For the fell-walker or fell-runner, it is mostly a means of rapid descent. But for a fine prospect of the sylvan beauty of this part of Borrowdale, with Derwentwater and its islets, there is nevertheless an amiable scramble to be made out of the rocks of Nitting Haws, White Rake and Blea Crag. These form a broad, stepped ridge, at times inconveniently covered in junipers, but enough rock is evident to retain interest and there is a good though distant view of the steeper cliffs of Goat Crag farther to the left across the intervening slope. You may even spot the odd rock-climber, but Goat Crag has also lost popularity except for a few 'starred' climbs.

Cross the bridge into Grange and take the track signed to Hollows Farm. When this swings uphill to the right take the left fork along the river bank to the camping area. There is also a field for camping on the right and good parking under the trees just beyond. A stile leads over the wall out of this field with a path heading straight up the hillside towards the lowest rocks. Easy scrambling over these amidst bracken leads to a steeper buttress but this is soon left behind by way of a rock ramp behind a holly on the left-hand side. A series of rocky knotts follows towards a prominent scree-slide and there are little rock scrambles camouflaged by junipers on either side of this, until a grass terrace is reached below a much steeper upper buttress. It is debatable which way to go next. Quite a long way to the right a heather-filled groove can provide one solution but I prefer to go left and scramble up rock and junipers to easier ground amidst heather. A little farther on is another little rock band found easiest at its right-hand end and finally a little rock nose effectively brings the scrambling to an end. I hope the increasingly rampant vegetation leaves enough visible rock for you to enjoy.

Ahead the general line of the ridge leads up to the tourist path along the fell top, but it is then more of a ramble. It would be a pleasant continuation to head northwards as far as Catbells – and look for Mrs Tiggywinkle's hiding place on the homeward path down to Grange.

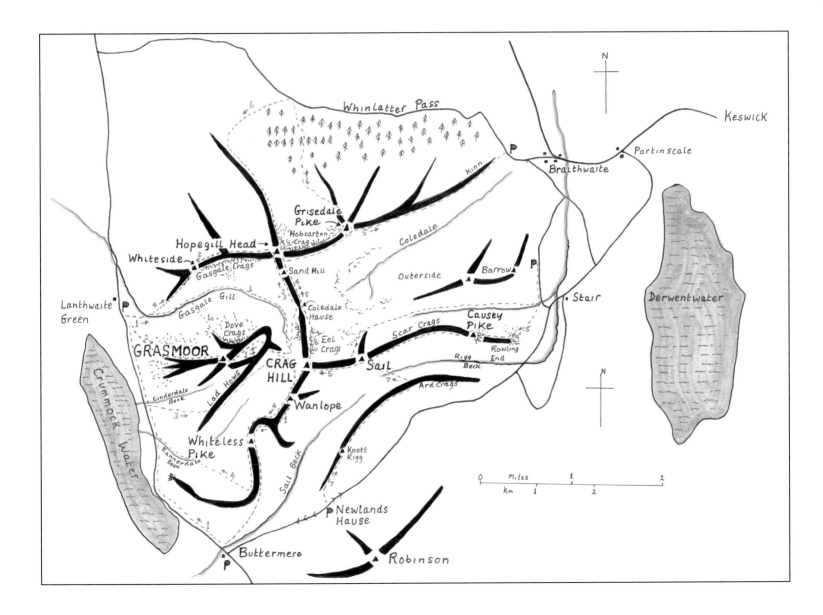

THE GRASMOOR GROUP

	Approximate Time	Star Rating	Assessment of Difficulty
1. Grasmoor via Gasgale Gill, Coledale Hause; return via Whiteless Pike	4 hours	*	—
1a. Variation: Grasmoor via Dove Crags	4 hours	—	—
2. Grasmoor direct from Lanthwaite Green; return via Gasgale Crags	4–5 hours	**	—
2a. Scramble on North West Shoulder of Grasmoor	add 1/2 hour	**	1–2
3. Grasmoor from Crummock Water; the Lad Hows Ridge	4 hours	*	—
4. Whiteside, Hopegill Head and Whiteless Pike: the western circuit of Grasmoor	5–6 hours	***	—
5. The Coledale Round: Causey Pike, Crag Hill and Grisedale Pike from Braithwaite	5 hours	***	—
6. Hopegill Head and Grisedale Pike from Whinlatter Pass	4–5 hours	*	—
7. Crag Hill via Knott Rigg and Ard Crags	4–5 hours	*	—

THE GRASMOOR GROUP

This most attractive group of fells is a sheer delight. Springy turf, fine ridges that link up in the most convenient ways, and splendid views – without too much of the more savage and rocky grandeur to be found farther south and west – make it a favourite for many fell-walkers. Bounded on the north by the Whinlatter Pass, by Crummock Water on the west, and on the south-west by the Braithwaite to Buttermere road over Newlands Hause, these hills certainly offer a good selection of enjoyable horseshoe ridge-walks. Grasmoor, Grisedale Pike, Hopegill Head, Crag Hill, Eel Crag, Causey Pike and Wanlope are the main peaks, and most walkers will want to tramp the ridges to climb them. The partial exception is Grasmoor, a huge mass of a mountain, whose most-seen aspect is from Crummock Water. From the lake it looks impressive but uninviting because

of its enormous scree slopes and apparently shattered crags. This impression is not altogether true, and I will therefore deal with Grasmoor first.

1. Grasmoor via Gasgale Gill, Coledale Hause; return via Whiteless Pike

This is probably the easiest and most straightforward way, avoiding any head-on challenge by nipping round to get to the top. There is good parking at Lanthwaite Green at the northern end of Crummock Water, and footbridges across the beck lead to a path shadowing the stream up the left-hand side of the defile of Gasgale Gill to emerge at the high-level pass of Coledale Hause.

Stay with the stream, which tinkles down the depression between Grasmoor and the steep and shaly slope of Eel Crag, for its course is the line of the footpath climbing south-west in the right direction. Near the col, the beck may become lost in peat hags but a path crosses the hause heading upwards and westwards and is the one to follow. In about a mile the summit cairn of Grasmoor is reached. If it's not too hazy, wide-ranging distant views in almost every direction are the reward.

From the summit of Grasmoor a very speedy descent and return to Lanthwaite Green is possible by descending the easy slopes due west to Grasmoor End and then plunging steeply south-west down the long and dry scree-slopes of Red Gill. For most enthusiasts this is certainly too fast and too fierce a way, and it curtails the enjoyment all too quickly. It is better to retrace your steps from the summit eastwards back to the col and so, by a good path, to the little peak of Wanlope with splendid views down to Buttermere. The rocky ridge of Whiteless Edge next leads out to Whiteless Pike, followed by grassy slopes towards Buttermere; a choice of parallel paths is offered and both head back north-west to Rannerdale A final walk along the road beside the lake eventually gets you back to the original starting point at Lanthwaite Green.

1a. Variation: Grasmoor via Dove Crags
This walk is a variation on the last one, allowing wider views at an earlier stage, but the path on the edge of Dove Crags is very sketchy.

Dove Crags is the name for the great semi-circular hollow scooped out of the northern flank of Grasmoor, but the crags and gullies – except in winter – are too shattered and loose to be of any interest to anybody other than a climber of suicidal tendencies. However they certainly look impressive, and this approach to Grasmoor has the merit of allowing the walker a good view of them, involving as it does, a tramp half-way up Gasgale Gill and then an upward struggle through heather to pick up the edge of the cirque. It is then a straightforward uphill walk on grass and moss along the edge of the crags to the summit plateau.

2. Grasmoor direct from Lanthwaite Green; return via Gasgale Crags
Rock-climbers on an off-day can tackle Grasmoor by way of Lorton Gully, the well-defined cleft facing north-west which is well seen from Lanthwaite Green. This is an entertaining expedition but probably beyond the sort of scrambling that any but the most experienced will wish to attempt.

There are, however, two other adjacent possibilities, a walk and a scramble, which both offer a direct way on to Grasmoor's summit. These ways go up the north-west shoulder of the mountain just to the north of Lorton Gully.

The start is not very promising, as a green pathway leads invitingly through bracken but then gives way to a tedious struggle up scree towards the lower rocks. There are, however, signs of a path, so don't be put off and as height is gained this path improves a little. A rocky gateway is the immediate objective and after passing through it the path heads up to the right to a little shoulder at about a thousand feet above the lake. Thankfully the screes are left behind and the path becomes better still, winding steadily upwards. Walkers should stick to the path, but it is on the edge of splendid little slabs, walls and rocky ledges that the scrambler will find almost irresistible entertainment.

Eventually at a second shoulder, overlooking a gully, the path swings away to the left and continues to Grasmoor End. This is not the summit, but it is only a gentle walk over springy turf to reach the summit cairn.

If the scrambling lower down whetted your appetite, there is more to be had. At the second shoulder, where the path leads to the left, a slender but broken ridge of rock rises to the right from the scree in the head of the gully. This provides a staircase for a hundred feet or so and then gives way to more little buttresses and walls until the footpath is again reached much nearer to Grasmoor End.

On one occasion two of us had completed this scramble and had walked beyond the summit to admire the fine views down Dove Crags and across to Gasgale Crags. We had put down our rucksacks while we fiddled with lenses and cameras when an extraordinarily powerful gust of wind nearly blew us both over the edge. With great difficulty we recovered our balance only to see both our rucksacks tumbling away down the deepest gully on Dove Crags. Mine of course was the heavier and I had an exasperating descent of five hundred feet or so to retrieve it, collecting the other sack en route.

This fine high-level excursion may be prolonged by walking over to Crag Hill summit or to Grisedale Pike. Whichever way you choose, the return via Coledale Hause, Sand Hill and the traverse along the excellent level ridge of Gasgale Crags and Whiteside is probably the most attractive way to return to Lanthwaite Green. This path is well marked and although steep, the descent is a speedy and exhilarating one, firstly down shale and then through bracken and heather.

Grasmoor seen from Crummock Water.

3. Grasmoor from Crummock Water; the Lad Hows ridge

Not quite as direct as the last route, this approach from Buttermere starting half-way along Crummock Water is nevertheless better than it looks from the valley. From Wanlope or Whiteless Pike, however, it is much more obvious that there is a clearly-defined ridge up the northern edge of Rannerdale Beck. The ridge most definitely exists, despite your doubts, and it forms a natural line of ascent. The starting point is Cinderdale Beck, the stream north of Rannerdale Beck, where there is pleasant camping. A faint path climbs eastwards towards the rounded end of Lad Hows, which looks from this angle like a separate hill. Once attained, however, the slender grassy ridge which connects Lad Hows to Grasmoor is apparent and it provides the logical way upwards, to arrive on the little col between Crag Hill and Grasmoor. Probably the most enjoyable walk from that point is to finish along Gasgale Crags before descending to Lanthwaite Green. Half a mile or so of road-walking will then get you back to your starting point.

4. Whiteside, Hopegill Head and Whiteless Pike: the western circuit of Grasmoor

An excellent walk, encircling Grasmoor itself – though a quick dash to the summit is of course also feasible. The starting point is once again Lanthwaite Green so you tramp off towards Gasgale Gill, but only for a short way, before crossing the stream by a footbridge and striking off uphill to the left through heather. A narrow path, which rapidly becomes more obvious, then picks a shaly way directly up the knobbly shoulder thrown down towards Lanthwaite Green by Gasgale Crags. As you climb higher, the great sweep of the crags becomes more and more apparent, too slaty and loose to be of value to the climber, but is no less dramatic for that.

I went that way one spring day in very curious wind conditions. At road level there was a stiff breeze, but a thousand feet higher it was so fierce that we literally could not stand up for more than a few seconds. And so we carried on uphill partly on hands and knees, grabbing at heather and rocks, trying to stand, and lurching about from one hold to another. The wind became fiercer and fiercer, and it developed into a real battle . . . indeed, a most exhilarating fight! Dust, heather-twigs, and little stones all flew past as we clawed our way upwards. Then, at about 2,500 feet, we realised that the intensity of the wind was decreasing markedly. It was only as we climbed the last two or three hundred feet to the end of the almost level ridge that we could once again stand normally. On the rocks of the ridge we sat in sunshine with only a slight breeze, but just below us there was still a ferocious stream of air battering away at the hillside. Perhaps the tunnel effect of Gasgale Gill has something to do with it.

The summit of Whiteside is really nothing more than a bump on the level ridge above Gasgale Crags, and you can walk on a pleasantly-exposed path along its crest, with fine views to the Solway Firth in the north, to reach Hopegill Head and Hobcarton Crag. The latter is reputed to be a botanist's delight, but if any botanists venture on to those crumbling walls without good ropes anchored firmly to the top rocks, they must have a lot of nerve. I don't think that the rare plants are in much danger of disturbance by humans.

There is an obvious continuation of the line of the ridge of Gasgale Crags heading over to Grisedale Pike, but that is for another day. Instead, a short descent and a climb up again to the south takes you over Sand Hill before a descent to Coledale Hause for a welcome drink from the little stream.

The next objective is Crag Hill by way of Eel Crag, and a sketchy path leads steeply up scree and rock going southwards up the edge of Eel Crag to the trig point on top of Crag Hill. Alternatively, for the direct route may look intimidating, you may more easily follow the course of the little stream mentioned earlier to reach the col between Grasmoor and Crag Hill, and then climb up to Crag Hill's summit. The views looking down Coledale and across to Skiddaw to the north-east are particularly dramatic.

Turning to the south-west, towards Buttermere, the ridge path leads out to Wanlope and then curves narrowly and gracefully out to Whiteless Pike. From there you look across Buttermere to the fine fells of the High Stile group, and can clearly work out how your descent is to be made. A first steep section goes down the broad south ridge, before swinging north-west again down the line of the beck leading to Rannerdale. Along the road a last tramp leads below the shattered crags and screes of Grasmoor.

5. The Coledale Round: Causey Pike, Crag Hill and Grisedale Pike from Braithwaite

This excellent circuit can be done successfully in either direction, dependent on whether you choose to gain height quickly to reach Causey Pike, or more gently to Grisedale Pike. Personally I prefer the former and so will describe the walk that way. It may also be worth pointing out to peak-baggers that you can, with a little more effort than the described walk bag six peaks of 2,500 feet or more (namely Sail, Hopegill Head, Grisedale Pike, Wanlope, Crag Hill and Grasmoor) all in one go. I generally find that it is best to park beside the unfenced back road about half-way between Braithwaite and Stonycroft/Stair, thus reducing the road walk at the end of the day.

Causey Pike is a most eye-catching peak, particularly from anywhere around Keswick, but the real ridge begins at Rowling End above the little hamlet of Stair. Although a well-marked path heads from Stair up the north-western flank of Causey Pike to its summit, a slightly steeper one heads directly up the rocky ridge of Rowling End and gets you quickly on your way with more perspiration but with increased interest. Continue to the pert little rocky summit of Causey Pike, where the line of the ridge ahead is revealed, beckoning the walker along the crest of Scar Crags, and then up a long slope to Sail (incidentally, from the hause just beyond it a good escape route path descends directly to Braithwaite). There is then a fine little exposed ridge to traverse, and a climb up a rocky stretch to the windy summit of Crag Hill.

I well remember one New Year's Day scrabbling about on all fours on ice-encrusted rocks on that little ridge, and then, as the snow-clouds thickened, having to lie on the ice behind my rucksack to get the correct compass-bearing for Coledale Hause.

Peak-baggers will rush off to do Wanlope and Grasmoor at this point, but instead head north above the sweep of Eel Crags and descend to Coledale Hause. The next stage is to skirt the shale of Sand Hill ahead and pick up the path that runs eastwards over Hobcarton Crags – and don't disturb any dangling botanists as you pass! – before toiling up to the summit of Grisedale Pike. The views can be very extensive, so long as you don't arrive just as mist obscures everything, especially the descent path. This heads down the north-east ridge towards the great conifer plantations on the side of the ridge of Kinn, where the footpath (which now avoids the lowers slopes to allow them to recover from erosion), leads to the car park a few yards up the Whinlatter Pass out of Braithwaite. From here it is a straightforward return to collect the car, glowing with memories of a grand day's walking.

6. Hopegill Head and Grisedale Pike from Whinlatter Pass

Carefully choose your parking place just off the Whinlatter Pass road (somewhere near Blaze Bridge perhaps), bearing in mind that the ridge you want is obvious enough, running north-north-west from Hopegill Head over Ladyside Pike towards you. Your ingenuity will suggest the easiest approach. Once the ridge itself is gained there is a bit of a track, but that is all, suggesting that this ridge is favoured more by sheep than humans. However, there is an entertaining section just before reaching Hopegill Head, where awkwardly-angled slabs of slaty and slippery rock make you ponder for a moment. However, no sooner are you aware of the difficulty than it is over, and you can scramble happily up to the cairn on Hopegill Head.

The way across to Grisedale Pike is perfectly obvious, and the north ridge of Hobcarton End heading back towards Whinlatter is equally obvious, though the descent down to the Forestry plantations does not invite a return journey in the upward direction. If you are lucky, the Forestry track you reach just before the road will be reasonably dry, and if not you'll be up to the ankles in mud. Don't worry, however, as it is only a quarter of a mile or so to where you left your dry footwear, and certainly don't let such minor considerations put you off what is a good and worthwhile walk.

7. Crag Hill via Knott Rigg and Ard Crags

For a good short day with a difference, leave your car at Newlands Hause and head up over Knott Rigg and Ard Crags, descend to the little col between Sail Beck and Rigg Beck, then go up a well-defined slanting track to the lowest point of the ridge between Sail and Crag Hill. You can then do the ridge, the summit, Wanlope and Whiteless Pike before descending by a fine grassy ridge back to Newlands Hause. The only painful bit will be on the little slog uphill right at the very end.

Right: From Dove Crags, Grasmoor, to Coledale Hause.
Overleaf left: Looking south-west over Wanlope from Eel Crag.
Overleaf right: View from Rowling End to (left to right) Ard Crags, Crag Hill, Sail and Causey Pike.

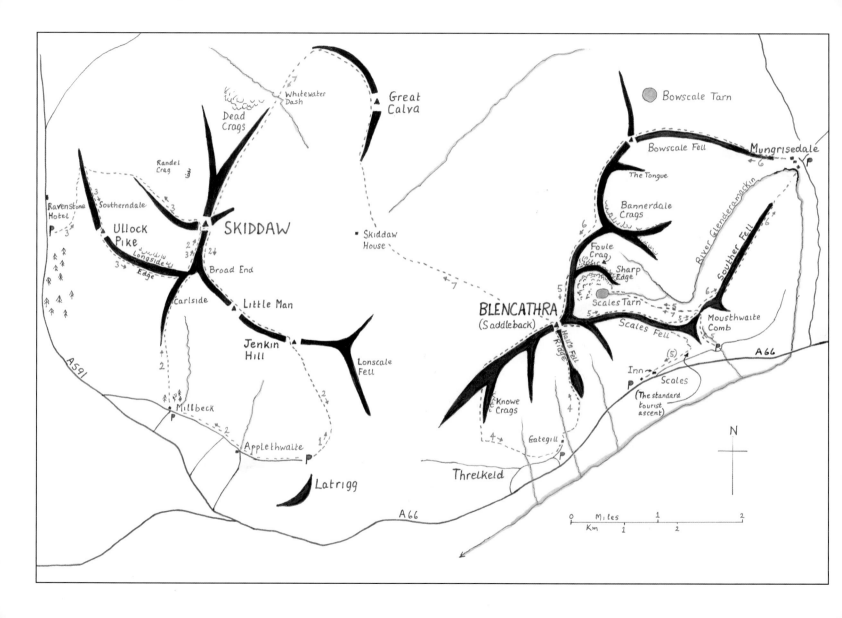

Whitewater Dash

Great Calva

Dead Crags

Randel Crag

Ravenstone Hotel

Southerndale

SKIDDAW

Skiddaw House

Bowscale Tarn

Bowscale Fell

The Tongue

Mungrisedale

Ullock Pike

Longside Edge

Broad End

Bannerdale Crags

River Glenderamackin

Carlside

Little Man

Foule Crag

Sharp Edge

Souther Fell

Jenkin Hill

Lonscale Fell

Scales Tarn

BLENCATHRA (Saddleback)

Scales Fell

Mousthwaite Comb

Millbeck

Hall's Fell Ridge

Inn

Scales

A66

A591

Applethwaite

Knowe Crags

Latrigg

Gategill

Threlkeld

(The standard tourist ascent)

A66

Miles

Km

N

SKIDDAW and BLENCATHRA GROUP

	Approximate Time	Star Rating	Assessment of Difficulty
SKIDDAW			
1. Via Latrigg and Jenkin Hill	3–4 hours	—	—
2. Via Mill Beck; return via Jenkin Hill	3–5 hours	*	—
3. Via Ullock Pike and Longside Edge	4–6 hours	***	—
BLENCATHRA			
4. Via Hall's Fell Ridge	3–5 hours	**	—
5. Via Scales Fell and Sharp Edge	3–5 hours	***	1
6. From the north via Bowscale Fell	5–6 hours	**	—
7. Traverse of Blencathra and Skiddaw via Great Calva	6–8 hours	***	—

SKIDDAW

Skiddaw is often dismissed by rock-climbers as a 'heap of tot' ('tot' being an abbreviation for 'tottering rubbish'), and it is true that it can in places seem like a pile of slippery slates. Certainly there seems to be no safe rock-climbing to be had on its crags; indeed the only crag of any size on the mountain is that above the Whitewater Dash waterfalls north of Skiddaw and that is aptly named 'Dead Crags'. Although Skiddaw has nothing worthwhile to offer the rock-climber, it has much to offer the walker. It is the fourth highest peak in the Lake District and, like the Matterhorn, which, when you are on it, also seems to be all loose rock, it is a very shapely mountain. It must also be one of the Lake District's most popular hills, possibly because it presents its very best aspect to the town of Keswick at its foot.

Seen in the late afternoon from any of the numerous viewpoints along Derwentwater or from the road up to Watendlath, with the setting sun throwing shadows across the ridges and valleys of its south face, Skiddaw indeed looks an attractive peak. Its ascent is particularly suitable for a fairly short day, or one with plenty of time for looking at the views, for none of the principal routes to the summit takes much more than a couple of hours and it is always fairly easy walking.

1. Skiddaw via Latrigg and Jenkin Hill

As an approach to such a big and handsome mountain, for a fit walker this route can only be described as a doddle. No doubt it was eminently suitable for the excursions on pony-back which were very popular a hundred years ago.

Many walkers nowadays avoid the early stages of the traditional approach, which curves round the western slopes of Latrigg and also provides some fine views across Derwentwater and up Borrowdale, by parking in the hollow behind Latrigg. The approach is simple enough, at the end of the continuation of the road from Applethwaite. On leaving the car park the path is also obvious, up the broad south-east slope. The climb is perhaps a little steeper than expected as far as Jenkin Hill, then the angle eases somewhat as the track skirts the summit of Little Man, masquerading for a while as the real summit. Finally, the south end of the broad summit ridge is reached and the highest point is a quarter of a mile farther north.

Unless your objective is solely to get to the top of Skiddaw by the easiest and fastest walking route, there are better ways to go.

2. Skiddaw via Millbeck; return via Jenkin Hill

This is a much better alternative to the previous boring trudge and it is started just behind Millbeck Farm where there is usually limited parking near by. A signed track leads up the west side of Millbeck and then follows the course of the gill all the way, steeply, to the hause where Carlside and Longside Edge meet Broad End. It is, however, a better way, because it is not so enclosed, to take the left fork in the path and head up the long spur that Carlside throws down towards Millbeck and which also has a good path up it. You climb two thousand feet in a mile as far as the hause, and can then enjoy fine views across the southern ridges of Skiddaw and to the north-west down Southerndale. A tiny, shallow tarn actually on the hause can locate the precise position in a mist. Then from the hause a slanting track rises five hundred feet up very slaty ground to reach the southern end of the summit ridge and although this is not the actual summit, it is a better viewpoint than the real one, which is just along the ridge.

Probably the best descent from the top, to make this into a good round, is to return to the south summit and then head down the broad pony-track to Jenkin Hill and so to the road behind Latrigg. Then you can marvel at the stamina of those fell-runners who can reach the summit of Skiddaw from Keswick by this route, up and down, in not much over an hour!

3. Skiddaw via Ullock Pike and Longside Edge

This is probably the most attractive way up the mountain because of the intrinsic interest in climbing a well-defined ridge at a steady angle, with fine views across Bassenthwaite and to the Buttermere fells. Parking isn't so easy on the main road, but once you've solved that problem (there are a couple of small lay-bys) the best starting point is just to the right (south) of the Ravenstone Hotel. A signed path climbs through conifers and then slants at an easier angle upwards to gain and

turn south along the long ridge leading through heather to Ullock Pike. The way goes along the slaty rocks of Longside Edge and the sense of exposure gets keener all the time as the edge sharpens a little. Eventually there is a little dip to the hause at the point where the paths from Carlside and Millbeck come in. A final effort is then needed, slanting upwards across the slates to the south summit, and along the level ridge to the north (main) summit.

The country to the north, the 'Back o' Skidda', is as unlike the south side as can be imagined. In fact it is much more akin to the 'Bostik-trot' stretches of the southern section of the Pennine Way, where the mud is like glue sucking your boots off and the man-eating heather devours the ankles of the unwary. It must have some sort of wild charm, however, for earlier generations have identified various points of land to the north of Skiddaw with the mockingly genital names of 'Broad End', 'Willy Knott', 'Cockup', 'Little Cockup' and 'Great Cockup'.

Unless the weather is uncertain, don't just return by your route of ascent. Instead, head north-west across untracked ground, skirting to the north of the broken rocks of Randel Crag and continue descending in a north-westerly direction. You will soon pick up the line of the broad ridge bounding Southerndale Beck and you can follow this, down heathery slopes and probably in near-solitude, until you can descend into Southerndale itself. Then pick a line across the toe of the Ullock Pike ridge and return to your starting point. Curlew, lapwing, sheep and the odd raven may watch your progress on this stretch, but it is unlikely that any human being will be in sight.

A longer alternative descent would be to stay with the path northwards over the summit of Skiddaw and descend to the waterfall at Whitewater Dash. From there the packhorse track of the Cumbria Way leads you north-west to Bassenthwaite.

I went this way once with some friends who were determined to climb Skiddaw. However, on the steeper bit going towards Ullock Pike they were going at a slower pace than suited me, since I had promised my wife that I would join her for some afternoon tea. Mist was coming in fairly rapidly but they insisted that they were all right and would turn back if the mist became too bad to see properly. They had maps and compasses, so with their assurances that we would all meet for tea I rushed off to the summit. I had intended to return by the route described above, but decided that, because of the mist and my lingering uncertainty about my

Right: Lonscale Fell and Skiddaw Little Man from Skiddaw summit.
Overleaf left: Skiddaw from the ice on Derwentwater.
Overleaf right: Blencathra from Castlerigg Stone Circle.

friends, I would return by almost exactly the route of my ascent. I did cut one corner and perhaps that explains why I missed them, but I didn't know that I had missed them for certain until I was practically back at the road. Half-reluctantly I headed for toast, tea and chocolate cake by the fire.

About five hours later, in the dark, they arrived. They had walked by mistake straight over the south summit above Broad End, down past Jenkin Hill to Latrigg. They then had to walk back along all those weary miles of road to collect the cars.

It's not the first time that a planned 'round' has turned into a traverse.

BLENCATHRA

Strangely, as we move two or three miles to the east, there is also an obvious change in the names, and these have the ring of Nordic sagas. The alternative name for this splendid mountain, Blencathra of Saddleback, is in a descriptive sense appropriate enough, but it has none of the magic. 'Glenderamackin', 'Glenderaterra' and 'Threlkeld' – two rivers and a village – along with Blencathra are names that belong to a different world. In names like those one can almost hear the elfin horns sounding across the great southern ridges that thrust symmetrically down into the Vale of Keswick from Blencathra's summit ridge, with their four deep gills gouged out between them. You can surely sense magic as you look to the mountain from the Castlerigg Stone Circle.

As you drive in from the M6, the outline of Sharp Edge, which provides one of the two most interesting routes up the mountain, is clearly visible. The views from the summit are very extensive because of its comparative isolation, particularly across to the Buttermere fells and to Clough Head and the Dodds ridge. It might not quite reach the 3,000-foot mark in terms of height, and like its neighbour Skiddaw it has no worthwhile rock-climbing, but its impact is great. This mountain certainly commands and deserves attention and respect from every mountaineer; for the fell-walker it is a gem.

4. Blencathra by Hall's Fell Ridge
This is arguably the best way up, though a vertical climb of 2,300 feet in a mile may seem daunting. However it is undeniably *the* direct way to the top – actually ending at the summit cairn.

The best approach is to take the northern turn off the A66 into Threlkeld, park along the first road on the right, then walk up the walled lane heading for Gategill. A signed footpath takes you just beyond the intake wall (beside a waterfall at the foot of Gategill) then a slaty path rises through bracken and slants north-north-east on to Hall's Fell. Soon the ridge sharpens, becoming rockier, then narrower and increasingly exposed as height is gained. It is quite an exciting way up and often it looks as though rock-climbing or scrambling will be required, particularly on the last steep bit near the summit, although in fact this is not the case. Hall's Fell is certainly not just a trudge. The little intricacies retain one's interest all the way up – and suddenly there in front of you is the summit cairn.

I once felt very pleased with myself because I went up Hall's Fell to the top from the road, and back to the road by the same route in reverse, in exactly sixty minutes. However I realised later that aspirants for the Bob Graham Round (the great Lakeland twenty-four hour mountain marathon) have also only got about an hour for the ascent – and that is after they've been more or less continuously on the move for eighteen hours or so. That put me in my place.

From the cairn the summit ridge beckons along its length. Vast, rolling, grassy slopes fall away to the north but are hardly noticed for the eye is inevitably held by the grandeur of the views down the great combes on the left and away to Borrowdale and Derwentwater, to Clough Head and the line of the Dodds ridge. Blencathra is so detached from other hills of comparable height that the views from it are consequently much more extensive.

There are no difficulties at all along the edge of the crags and the shoulder is soon reached where Knowe Crags forms the bounding edge of the south face of the mountain. A steep but easy path now descends grassy slopes, but when it swings west take the left fork (south-east) and so reach the intake wall. The continuing path on the north side of this quickly returns you to Gategill.

Whichever way you climb Blencathra, do try to avoid the Blease Fell–Knowe Crags path as a way of ascent, for there are two thousand feet of upward trudge with no worthwhile views.

I did once climb this mountain by way of Blease Fell and lost one of my dogs in a mist that developed on the summit. Unfortunately I didn't realise he wasn't with me until I was back in the valley, so I had to repeat the whole process and go back up and down all over again searching for him. In the event he didn't turn up for a few days, but the experience was enough to confirm my opinion about the inferiority of this edge of the mountain as a way up.

5. Blencathra by Scales Fell and Sharp Edge

Justifiably popular, this particular way up the mountain is a splendid walk, whilst the scrambling on Sharp Edge adds spice and sometimes excitement to the day.

Rather than parking on the lay-bys just off the A66 at Scales, I suggest you drive about half a mile along the metalled track that continues beyond the White Horse Inn towards Southerfell and Mungrisdale. There is normally parking available for some cars just round an elbow bend, immediately before the first fell gate across the road. A path then leads above the left bank of the stream emerging from Mousthwaite Comb and quickly joins a good track slanting across the left side the Comb to reach a little col above the River Glenderamackin.

The sudden upthrust of Sharp Edge is now normally clearly visible ahead to the north-west. Take a sharp left (west) turn on the col, and follow a good and almost level path for half a mile with the Glenderamackin rushing parallel below. Now follow a short climb upwards again, bearing left, then crossing the beck. This is the outflow from Scales Tarn, which is hidden in the combe above. The path follows the right bank to reach it. This is a good place for a welcome rest before heading up the slope to the base of the narrow ridge that is Sharp Edge.

One path follows the crest, while another skirts below it. Those thinking that the sheltered lower path is a softer option are only partly right; it is indeed usually sheltered from the wind, but it reaches a point where an upward scramble is clearly necessary to join the path along the crest. Whichever path you chose, the first 'interesting bit' now lies in wait. This involves a delicate step across a flat slab, with quite a drop below and a scarcity of handholds. It is easy when it's dry and you move confidently, but wet slaty rock can make it feel more frightening (and wet slate tends to be slippery.) However, it is quickly over and huge holds reached at the point where Sharp Edge itself runs into the slaty grooves of Foule Crag. A few steps slanting upwards to the right from here should lead into the main groove trending back left, up which you make further upward progress. Then a side step to a slighter groove soon brings easier ground into reach. While easy when dry, these grooves become much more awkward when wet or with any ice about.

On the other hand, I do not want to put anybody off! I recently watched a white husky (recently returned from a trans-Antarctic crossing, I was told) almost fly along Sharp Edge and up Foule Crag. My little son did most of it on his own legs when he was only three (admittedly an age when kids know no fear) but even my wife, who doesn't like climbing a three-foot ladder, has been up it – under protest of course!

Once Foule Crag is behind you, the summit cairn on Blencathra, with Hall's Fell dropping south immediately below it, is a quarter of a mile farther on.

Unless you intend to either traverse the mountain or descend by one of the other southern ridges, you should now retrace your steps back towards Sharp Edge. However, well before reaching it, turn south-east down a slope that leads quickly to the very attractive, curving, grassy ridge on the upper part of Scales Fell. Here you join, for part of the way, the 'standard' or 'tourist' path, which has been bulldozed into shape in the recent past. Somewhat to my own surprise, I believe that the result is an improvement on the older path, particularly for drainage, and that it will very quickly blend into the surroundings. If you should happen to stay on this path, you will be led down to Scales and the White Horse Inn. This may be an attractive option, but it was not your starting point. To regain *that* easily you should leave the ridge and this path and head off to the left (eastwards) to rejoin the col at the head of Mousthwaite Comb and so back to the parking place.

I realise that, in my enthusiasm to get to grips with Sharp Edge, I have omitted what I have called the 'tourist' path (no slur intended, for it is in fact a very good one.) After all, there could be many perfectly good reasons for *not* doing Sharp Edge: heavy rain, ice, high winds, a nervous disposition, maybe even a hangover from the night before (although that's a poor one). So to find it, this time parking is best sought on the large lay-bys beside the A66, just west of the White Horse Inn at Scales. Then the path is soon found slanting north-eastwards, behind the pub, up Scales Fell and rising to a point where it peers over into Mousthwaite Comb. The narrow path skirting the upper edge of the Comb is now officially discouraged because of erosion and the preferred one changes direction here to head generally westwards up the broad end of Scales Fell, soon reaching the sharper part. From this there are wonderful views across Blencathra's other fine ridges, then the path leads nicely to the top of the mountain.

Sharp Edge and Foule Crag, Blencathra.

6. Blencathra from the north via Bowscale Fell

More of a 'wild walk', because you will meet few others doing it, this is a surprisingly enjoyable day. The starting and finishing point is the little hamlet of Mungrisdale, reached by a secondary road off the A66, almost halfway between Penrith and Keswick. Parking is best just beyond the hamlet, past the sign for 'Mungrisdale Common', near the point where the road forks for Hutton Roof. Directly opposite this junction a track leads past a couple of houses, past a little quarry, then a good path immediately climbs rightwards uphill through bracken, gorse and rocky outcrops on to the broad end of Bowscale Fell. The path remains clear through bilberry and heather and as height is gained the rim of Bannerdale Crags is visible above the spur of the intervening Tongue. Before following the curve of the moor to reach the cairn on Bowscale Fell, do peep down the northern slope to spy Bowscale Tarn below, hidden from the valley. From the plateau the line of the ridge over and above Bannerdale Crags is well defined, if occasionally boggy, and the northern slope of Foule Crags, which is mostly weathered shale, is eventually reached. Climb upwards at right-angles to Sharp Edge (though you could of course make a flanking descent to reach and climb this instead, if you've the energy!) and so on to Blencathra's summit. The return is either back by the way you came or, much better, either down Sharp Edge or the ridge of Scales Fell to reach the little col at the head of Mousthwaite Comb. From there a short climb northwards on to the ridge of Southerfell leads back to Mungrisdale, bearing sharp right towards the foot of the ridge to reach the side road and the bridge over the Glenderamackin near the pub. It's then, as my mother used to say, 'nobbut a cock-stride' back to the car.

7. Traverse of Blencathra and Skiddaw via Great Calva

This is obviously one of the longest days to be enjoyed fell-walking in this area. It could be made even longer by starting from Mungrisdale and including Bowscale Fell as well as Blencathra and Skiddaw. The normal traverse is a splendid day anyway.

On a longer walk such as this it seems natural to fit in the best bits of any shorter ones you may have already done. So my starting point would undoubtedly be Mousthwaite Comb, before climbing up to Scales Tarn and then by Sharp Edge to Blencathra's summit. However going to the summit is really only to touch the cairn for luck. It is then best to return towards the top of Foule Crag in order to pick a line across the great moor of Mungrisdale Common ahead. A very broad-domed ridge heads just to the north of the rising springs of Roughton Gill and Sinen Gill (which both empty into the Glenderaterra Beck) and in a direct line north-westwards towards Great Calva. You may choose to stay on this course, crossing the Caldew en route and toiling up the very exhausting heathery slopes where they are at their steepest and the heather at its most voracious, to reach the top of Great Calva. However, from the experience of doing this walk in both directions, I would recommend a deviation from this stern line. Head a little farther west and get on to the bridle-way that runs north from Skiddaw House. Although I believe that this is a Youth Hostel, a staging post on the route of the Cumbria Way, this is a strange place, like an oasis in a desert of grass and heather-covered dunes. I've never been very close to it, feeling always that anybody who wanted to build a house in the midst of such a lonely, wild country must value privacy and be unlikely to welcome nosy parkers, but as it stands there, isolated amidst its windblown trees, it is an unmistakable landmark.

About half a mile beyond Skiddaw House there is a ridge of sorts coming down from Great Calva and there is a vague path coming down the ridge. It is a lot easier going up this way than the steeper and more direct one. When you reach the top there is no great view but a much more noticeable path becomes evident, swinging towards Little Calva and then descending fairly steeply down the line of a fence. It reaches the bridle-path again, just by the waterfalls of Whitewater Dash. The rocks of Dead Crags peer down at you from the ridge to Skiddaw, which is the way you must climb.

A steady pull up the north ridge of Skiddaw on the well-used path soon leads to the summit cairn and when you reach the other one on the top of Broad End you will once again see the Lakeland panorama below. Whichever way you choose to descend will depend on your transport arrangements. The best is certainly Longside Edge and Ullock Pike. On reaching civilisation again you may reflect with satisfaction on a day of mountain contrasts that is unusual in these hills.

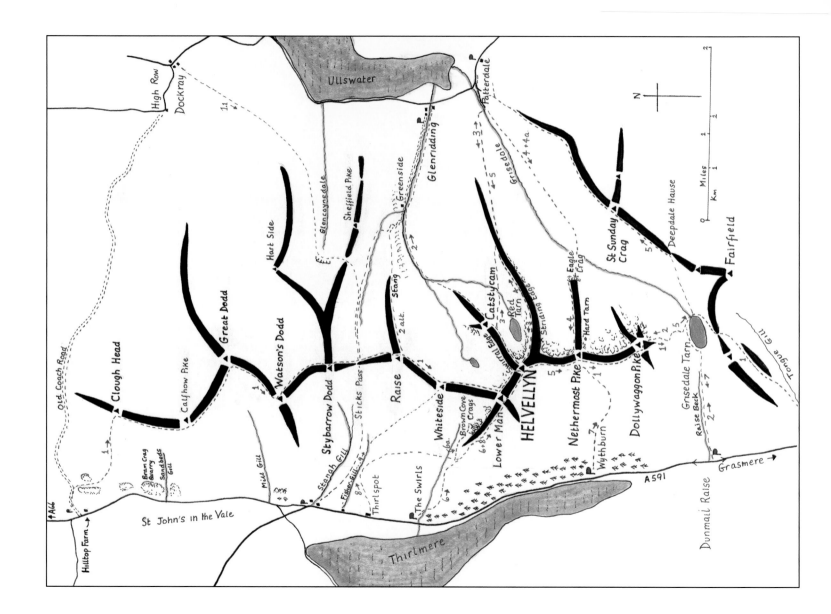

THE HELVELLYN GROUP

		Approximate Time	Star Rating	Assessment of Difficulty
1.	Traverse of the Dodds ridge: Clough Head, Raise and Helvellyn, descent to Grasmere down Tongue Gill	5–7 hours	**	—
1a.	Alternative start to Dodds Traverse from Dockray	5–7 hours	*	—
2.	From Dunmail Raise: Helvellyn to Glenridding Traverse	4–5 hours	**	—
3.	Helvellyn by Striding Edge and Swirral Edge from Patterdale	3–4 hours	***	1
4.	Helvellyn via Eagle Crag, Grisedale and Nethermost Pike; descent via Striding Edge	4–5 hours	**	1
4a.	Optional scramble on Eagle Crag en route	add 1/2 hour	*	3
5.	The Helvellyn Horseshoe	6 hours	***	—
6.	To Helvellyn via Helvellyn Gill, Brown Cove Crags and Lower Man	3–5 hours	—	—
6a.	Alternative scramble on Brown Cove Crags	add 1 hour	**	3
7.	Helvellyn from Wythburn via Nethermost Pike, descent via Raise Beck	3–5 hours	—	—
8.	Helvellyn from Thirlspot	4–6 hours	—	—
8a.	Alternative scramble (or footpath) via Fisher Gill	4–6 hours	**	2
9.	Other possible gill scrambles in the area	—	—	—

THE HELVELLYN GROUP

I have been tramping the fells and ridges of Helvellyn for nearly fifty years and have never got bored with them. In fact my enthusiasm grows rather than diminishes as the years pass, and a sparkling winter's day will still find me rushing over to Patterdale, or up Raise Beck to Grisedale Tarn, so as to make the most of the exhilarating walking and fine views. The finest combes or coves are, as usual, on the eastern side of the main ridge and most of the best walks consequently start or finish on that side. The western side of the range, overlooking Thirlmere, is generally not so interesting and there are not many jewels hidden amongst the Helvellyn screes above the dense conifer treeline. That is not to say, however, that all of the western side is as tedious as a superficial acquaintance might suggest, and there are some pleasant surprises. One really good long walk, which traverses the whole of the main ridge, is an excellent starting point.

1. Traverse of the Dodds ridge: Clough Head, Raise and Helvellyn; descent to Grasmere down Tongue Gill

This really is a marvellous day's fell-walking, increasing in interest and building up to a climax on Helvellyn if you start at the northern end. It is well worthwhile making the necessary transport arrangements.

I used to approach the ridge by way of Bramcrag Quarry but old footpaths are now closed and even the dreadful route via Fisher's Wife's Rake (which I admit I failed to identify properly for years) is not accessible. It is best to either park or be dropped off at the western end of the unsurfaced old coach road to Matterdale, which is at the northern end of the B5322 road running through St John's in the Vale. (There is a sign: 'Matterdale unsuitable for motors', GR 316231.) This old road leads past Hill Top Farm, forking left, then watch for a stile over the fence on the right and further stiles between Hilltop Quarries to get on to open fell. A path climbs in a groove from here to the south-east, then zigzags through the steeper ground of Red Screes (not to be confused with those at the top of Kirkstone Pass) and so to the trig point and windbreak on Clough Head. From here a gentle descent over grassy ground along the broad ridge top leads to the little rock outcrop of Calfhow Pike.

For anyone wishing to omit Clough Head, just before the last part of the ascent to Red Screes, leave the path and head for a prominent rock spike on the right. A narrow path behind this gives an exhilarating little traverse above Wanthwaite Crags to reach Jim's Fold (sheepfold). From here grass slopes will take you to Calfhow Pike.

Beyond Calfhow Pike the line to take up the long slope south-east towards Great Dodd is obvious enough, being marked with stones and cairns. However, as the summit gets within reach, the main path veers to the right towards Watson's Dodd and it is obvious that many walkers avoid the last short climb to Great Dodd's summit. Who Watson was, whose name was given to the next summit, distinguished only by a few stones, is not clear; but again the path – or is it just a sheep track? – carefully avoids the actual summit as it heads for Stybarrow Dodd.

Stybarrow Dodd sends out a long grassy spur to the east to Greenside and the old mines above Ullswater, and its summit is a rounded, grassy dome of no great distinction in itself. However, a rapid descent due south from the top, via a faint footpath, brings you to the highest point of the Sticks Pass. There is boggy ground immediately ahead on the gentle climb towards the rocks of the summit of Raise, while to the east there is a wide depression, which used to hold snow for many

months. I had many splendid winter days skiing in this area in the years when we had snow that lasted, although I admit that it was a slog carrying skis all the way up there from Greenside. From the broken rocks on Raise onwards, it is clear that the easy, rolling grassy slopes of the Dodds have been left behind and sterner country is ahead. Catstycam stands proudly across Keppel Cove and a short descent from Raise, followed by a climb up to Whiteside, shows the sharper ridge ahead rising to Helvellyn Lower Man. Within minutes you are on Helvellyn's summit, with its fine views in all directions, especially down the impressive lines of Swirral Edge and Striding Edge, to Ullswater and High Street and back the way you've come, with Blencathra on the distant skyline. Apart from being a fine walk so far, I recall this being even better as a fell-run, for you can make marvellously fast progress along the rolling fells of the Dodds.

It is highly unlikely that you will have the summit of Helvellyn to yourself. The summit plateau has seen all sorts of antics over the years, from Morris dancing to an aeroplane landing (there is a little plaque up there to commemorate this latter event).

Heading south towards Nethermost Pike, High Crag and Dollywaggon Pike, the broad motorway path carefully avoids the best views in favour of the most level walking. It is much more rewarding to stay as close as you can to the edge of the crags, where there are excellent views down Nethermost Cove and Ruthwaite Cove. Just beyond Dollywaggon Pike you will need to join the main track again for the now improved zigzag descent to Grisedale Tarn. Finally there is the little climb up to Grisedale Hause and the descent, which is best taken by the old packhorse road and Little Tongue Gill to Grasmere.

1a. Alternative start to Dodds Traverse from Dockray

Normally you really do need to have a long-suffering, or non-walking, partner to take charge of the transport on a traverse, but if you start at Dockray, on the Ullswater side of the Helvellyn–Dodds ridge, you may have a fine day over the best of the same ground and descend to Patterdale, thus almost giving you a round. To return, I'd be inclined to hitch a lift.

From the maps it looks tempting to drive beyond Dockray to High Row and Dowthwaitehead, then walk from there to join the ridge at Great Dodd. The price paid, however, is that of a rather dreary trudge up the north flank of (the other) Deepdale to get there. It isn't worth it. Instead start at Dockray and head south-west, to the west (right) of the lump of Round How on to Watermillock Common

and get on to the Ullswater side of the ridge. The footpath leads to Swineside Knott and Brown Hills above Glencoyne Park; and the views along the beautiful lake of Ullswater, which are what justify this walk, are enchanting. The footpath contours under the broken crags at the head of Glencoynedale and then joins the Sticks Pass track, which may be followed upwards to the hause, in which case the Dodds will be missed out altogether. Now follow the gentle climb to the broken rocks on the summit of Raise and so over to Helvellyn. Depending on time and energy the return may be made either to Patterdale by way of Dollywaggon Pike and Grisedale or to Glenridding via Swirral or Striding Edge. (Later walks in this chapter cover these alternatives in more detail.)

2. From Dunmail Raise: Helvellyn to Glenridding Traverse

I know that two traverses one after the other is a bit extravagant, but this walk really is worth doing. There is easy parking just off the main road, and then the first bit is a steady uphill tramp up the steep-sided Raise Beck from Dunmail Raise, to the welcome sight of Grisedale Tarn as the angle eases. The next stretch is harder work, up the zigzag path sloping up to the ridge as it curves up to Dollywaggon Pike. It's well worth the effort and the views down Cock Cove, Ruthwaite Cove and then Nethermost Cove are superb. It is also well worth while skirting the very edge of the crags on Nethermost Pike to get a really good view of the splendid ridge that is Striding Edge, with its procession of walkers looking like an army of ants scurrying along its length.

The main footpath steers well away from the exposed ground towards the summit plateau and you will need to make a small detour to inspect the monument to Charles Gough, which is a plaque located at the point where the last upthrust of Striding Edge merges into the summit plateau. Times have certainly changed since Gough died and it was, so the story goes, three months before his body was found, still guarded by his faithful dog. However, the almost immortal hills remain and, apart from the vanished forests in the valleys, the views are essentially as the Romans or the Celts must have seen them thousands of years ago, and they are still wonderful.

There is a four-sided stone windbreak just a few feet lower than the summit on Helvellyn, which is a handy place for lunch, while a few yards farther along the summit plateau a cairn marks the point where Swirral Edge descends. Make up your mind whether you have time and energy for the longer way over to Lower Man and the descent down to Glenridding from Raise, or whether you will go down by way of Swirral Edge and Catstycam via Red Tarn Beck to pick up the path descending to Glenridding.

If you choose the longer way, head north over Lower Man to Whiteside, until a path heads off north-east and skirts above Red Screes and Keppel Cove, before descending steeply to Glenridding Beck. You may, however, find it more interesting to go just that bit farther beyond Whiteside and climb Raise. From its summit you may descend its stony shoulder to the north-east, instead of going down the Sticks Pass. The old ski-hut (if it is still there) should soon be in view and you'll find a good path from it going over Stang and joining the Sticks Pass at the top of the long zigzags that lead you down to the old Greenside mines. It is not particularly enjoyable tramping down the rutted track from there, but a footbridge spans the stream just above the old mine-workings and leads to a much more attractive path. This eventually goes round to Grisedale but before then it will take you nicely down to Glenridding with the absolute minimum of tarmac.

3. Helvellyn by Striding Edge and Swirral Edge from Patterdale

There is no doubt that the glory of Helvellyn is Striding Edge and every fell-walker wants to have walked that sharp crest at least once. Its existence is what almost certainly makes Helvellyn the most popular of all the Lakeland peaks and in summer the procession of walkers along it can be almost bewildering. But don't let that put you off, even if your own opportunity happens to be a fine summer's day, for this short round is still worth doing.

The start of this walk used to be easier but nowadays one can't park any more just off the metalled road opposite the end of the ridge (at GR 383153). Instead start down in the valley nearer to Patterdale and then walk up the road for a good half mile, before turning right at the gate across the road. Then cross Grisedale Beck and follow the track up the lower slope of the fellside opposite. It is a steady pull up the improved path and then a last sharp rise leads to the stile over the wall that has been in view for a long time. Suddenly there are rocks ahead and the path clambers over them. Bleaberry Crag, Low Spying How and High Spying How are the names given to them on the map, but to most people they all become merged into Striding Edge. There are views on both sides of the ridge, whereas before there was only the view across to Red Tarn and Swirral Edge enclosing it on the other side. In fine weather it seems almost impossible that anyone could fall off this rocky but broad path and be killed. Go up in winter though and you'll understand how it can happen.

On a grey day years ago I once left Grisedale with some friends for 'a quick dash up Striding Edge and down Swirral'. In the valley it was almost warm. There was little wind and, as can so easily happen, some of our party were lulled into a false sense of security. As we reached Striding Edge the greyness was transformed into a whirling, howling world of driving snow and ferocious wind, with almost nil visibility. It can take only a few minutes to become completely chilled under such conditions and one of our party was in jeans and had neither gloves nor hat of any kind, apart from his anorak hood. We had, of course, already really gone too far by the time we realised that he just hadn't got any spare clothing in his rucksack and it took all our combined spare clothes to get him safely down again before hypothermia took its toll. One slip under such circumstances could of course have been fatal.

On a fine day, however, there is only one bit that needs a little care and that is at the end of the level, rocky section, before the last rise up an eroded slope to the summit plateau. If in doubt at that point you can always retreat a little and find an easier way to bypass the bad section.

Once on the top, you may stroll around nonchalantly until you feel it is time to descend Swirral Edge. A large cairn, just beyond the O.S. triangulation point marking the actual summit, indicates the top of the rocks encircling Red Tarn below and also the way down. A few moments of care may be needed near the top, but you are soon on a good path that skirts under the conical summit of Catstycam. It then crosses the outflow from Red Tarn and then the boggy slopes to the end of the Striding Edge ridge. From there you may reverse your route of ascent back to the pains and pleasures of civilisation.

4. Helvellyn via Eagle Crag, Grisedale and Nethermost Pike; descent via Striding Edge
4a. Optional scramble on Eagle Crag en route.
Try this route as a splendid alternative to the more popular paths over Helvellyn. As is so often the case, just because the immediate approach is not completely obvious, many walkers who would thoroughly enjoy a tramp such as this fail to notice the possibility.

Park near Patterdale or Glenridding, or at the lower end of the Glenridding road if you can find a space, then walk up the road to the gate across it (GR 383157) at the old parking space opposite the end of the Striding Edge ridge. Beyond the gate continue up Grisedale on the metalled road for about a mile until the track for Grisedale Tarn then heads to the left of the second plantation. While passing this, the rocks of Eagle Crag and the broad ridge beyond, stretching up to Nethermost Pike, are clearly in view, with old mine spoil-heaps at the base of the rocks. This is the general line of the route.

If you don't feel in the mood for any scrambling you will have to head a little farther to the right of the foot of the ridge to avoid the rock walls and so climb up by grassy slopes and easy rakes to the top of Eagle Crag, where the rocky east ridge of Nethermost Pike is joined.

However, if you are in the mood for a scramble, it will be fairly obvious that the rocks to the left of the straight gully or gash that separates the two halves of the large main crag are for rock-climbers only. Fortunately, just to the right of the gully is a staircase of slabs which, if dry, will enable you to gain height on good rock, after which it is a case of following your own nose to find either the most interesting way up, or the easiest, bearing leftwards as you get above the top of the gully to reach easy ground.

The rocky ridge that stretches ahead looks very impressive, though in fact once you are on it there is really just good, rough walking and no actual scrambling is involved. As height is gained, just before the last pull on to the ridge, you will notice the glint of water, where the tiny Hard Tarn lies on a rocky shelf, under the steep rocks that buttress the ridge on the left. Incidentally, these rocks form a series of ledges split by incipient gullies and I had a surprisingly good ice-climbing day fighting a way up them in a blizzard.

As you reach the top of the ridge and gain Nethermost Pike your eye will be drawn to Striding Edge on the right across the combe. It will shortly provide you with a superb way down, particularly if you stay on its sharp crest.

A rapid descent down the main track to the metalled road can be varied by a diversion on the footpath through Brownend plantation to the pretty little Lanty's Tarn with a view over Ullswater. It will provide a fitting end to a really fine day on Helvellyn.

Right: Catstycam from the end of Striding Edge.
Overleaf left: Helvellyn summit with walkers descending Swirral Edge. Blencathra is in the background.
Overleaf right: Red Tarn and Striding Edge, Helvellyn.

5. Helvellyn Horseshoe

One of the problems of carving up the Lake District into chapters or regions is that it is all too easy to forget those walks which overlap two or more of the sections. The Helvellyn Horseshoe is just one such, and it should certainly be on your list. As with all the rounds there is a choice which way to go but my choice would be the anti-clockwise direction, because it is less of a toil from Grisedale Tarn up to Deepdale Hause than it is to slog up Dollywaggon Pike from the same tarn.

So begin in Patterdale and climb via Striding Edge to the summit of Helvellyn. A good early start will get you away in front of the crowds. Then follow the plateau edge round to Nethermost Pike and on to Dollywaggon Pike before descending to Grisedale Tarn. This feels like a painful loss of height gained, but console yourself with the thought that the direct track down Grisedale is very stony and uncomfortable indeed, particularly in its upper parts. So gird up your loins, not to speed across the desert like Daniel, but to climb the steadily rising and good path that leads diagonally from Grisedale Tarn up to Deepdale Hause, joining it at the dip where the path rises to Cofa Pike on the right-hand side (south-west) and to St Sunday Crag on the left (north-east). From that point you should get a good view back to Grisedale Tarn and Dollywaggon Pike.

It is then a steady uphill walk to the stony wilderness at the top of St Sunday Crag, followed by the gradual descent back along the good path and track down Black Crag and through the trees to join the road again at the gate, a quarter of a mile from Patterdale.

And there, in a few rather bald words, is a summary of what must rate as one of the 'top twenty' walks in the Lake District. The only reason why I have not said a great deal more is because its component parts have already been described earlier.

Helvellyn from the West (Thirlmere) Side

I would risk straining both my own imagination and your credulity if I were to seriously suggest that routes to Helvellyn from Thirlmere are in the same league of excellence as those on the east. Furthermore it is not so easy to make good 'rounds'. However, the creation of better parking places at Wythburn and at Helvellyn Gill (opposite the viewpoint over Thirlmere, where the road north emerges from the trees) plus the popularity of the camping spot and welcome refreshment at the King's Head at Thirlspot, all no doubt make it more than ever attractive to go up Helvellyn from the west. In addition, for a family walk, without getting involved in any of the potential risks of the ridges on the east side, the paths on this side do provide safe ways to the top of England's most popular 3,000-foot mountain. Once on top, the glory of those splendid views is just as much yours as it belongs to those who may have scaled fearsome crags to reach the same place. Perhaps surprisingly, there are even some exciting moments for competent scramblers.

Obviously an ascent by one of these paths can be followed by the descent of another, depending on how your transport is arranged or how much road-walking you are prepared to do at the end of the day.

6. To Helvellyn via Helvellyn Gill, Brown Cove Crags and Lower Man

At the point where the main road north along Thirlmere leaves the forest and trends away from the lake, there is a large viewpoint and parking place (often with an ice cream van), overlooking Thirlmere. On the other side of the road, by courtesy of the North West Water Authority, is a larger car park (the Swirls). This is the starting point for what is now surely the most popular walk up Helvellyn from the western side. It is straightforward and probably the shortest, which are no doubt its chief merits, if the objective is simply to climb the mountain.

The route starts at the edge of the forest, goes for a way up and to the right of the line of Helvellyn Gill and then heads up the unrelenting slope to the blunt end of Brown Cove Crags. Happily, new zigzags, aimed at reducing erosion, are making this first section less of a toil than it used to be. From the top of Brown Cove Crags the walk becomes much more pleasurable, skirting the edge of the cove and rapidly climbing to Helvellyn Lower Man and then the main summit.

Most walkers seem to return by reversing the ascent, though a longer variation may be made by descending via Whiteside down to Thirlspot using the old path that skirts the edge of Fisher Gill. The excellent possibility of the gill itself is mentioned later in this chapter.

Brown Cove can offer good skiing in the right conditions (although plenty of deep snow is needed for there are many boulders) and I have several times carried skis up to the main ridge and then had a good run down the line of Helvellyn Gill.

6a. Alternative scramble on Brown Cove Crags

Instead of following the main path up the end of Brown Cove Crags, take another path leading into the cove itself. The rocks are then arrayed on the right-hand side with an obvious main buttress in the centre of the crags. There is a broad terrace at the base of this buttress and a long broken rib of rock, also marked by a cairn, is the start of the scramble. This rib narrows higher up and ends on the right of an obvious steep corner crack, about a third of the way up the buttress.

Starting from the cairn there is a bit of fiddling about as you go right and then up left to get on to the rib, but this is then the means of gaining about 200 feet in height. It ends in a grassy gully just right of the steep corner crack that was visible lower down. Escape is possible leftwards but press on up the right-hand rake towards the skyline. This ends below a steep tower of rock, about twenty feet high, which appears to bar the way completely. However, a little ledge leading between some rocks on the right enables the corner to be turned and then an easy crack (not the short chimney with the jammed stone) leads back left towards the tower. A few feet are gained and there is 'Riley's Window', a hole through wedged blocks which leads excitingly but easily above the difficulties. Above are two grooves on the right of a large block and these lead to a grassy rake, a series of rather shattered rock ridges and a final grassy arete. Judiciously-placed cairns at three places on the

Riley's Window   BROWN COVE CRAGS

way up indicate the line of each section, so there should be no danger of wandering too far. The Helvellyn footpath is then only a few paces away.

There is no difficulty at all on this route for an experienced scrambler, though dry conditions are very advisable, as the rock remains greasy in the lower sections after rainy periods.

7. Helvellyn from Wythburn via Nethermost Pike; descent via Raise Beck

This is a bit less of a trudge than the normal path from Helvellyn Gill, although it is a little longer. There is a good car park on the right of the A591 heading north just past Wythburn church, near the southern end of Thirlmere; and the path goes from there, heading pleasantly up through the forest. Leaving the trees it contours around at an easier angle for a while above the head of Comb Gill, then toils up the fellside, carefully avoids Nethermost Pike and finally reaches the summit of Helvellyn. It is a safe and well-trodden way to get to the top. (I carried my son on my back that way before he was one year old and completed the Dodds Traverse as well. He slept for most of the way.)

Although you will probably reverse your way up to get back down again, you can make more of the day by heading south from the summit to Dollywaggon Pike, descending to Grisedale Tarn and then following the line of Raise Beck back to Dunmail Raise. Avoid tramping down the rather busy and dangerous A591 main road back to Wythburn by using the footpath on its east (right) side (you'll spot the footbridges). These lead to a forest track, so that one may stroll pleasantly back through conifers fragrant with resin.

8. Helvellyn from Thirlspot

To most walkers Thirlspot will be identified with the popular King's Head Inn on the right of the A591 road going north alongside Thirlmere towards Keswick. There is refreshment, parking and nearby camping; these are all good reasons, no doubt, why this is the start of a good way up Helvellyn.

The most obvious path, marked with fading white paint-flashes on the rocks, starts from behind the inn, and it goes at first north-east towards the Sticks Pass. However it soon swings back south-east in an upward slant across the fellside and before long joins the well-marked path going up the edge of Brown Cove Crags, that started up Helvellyn Gill. Its advantage is that it gains height more gently in

Brown Cove Crags from Helvellyn Lower Man.

the early stages and also enables a different return to be made down the steeper path to the car park at the bottom of Helvellyn Gill. The walk down to Thirlspot is on a reasonably safe stretch of the main road and, if your timing is good, you'll be well-placed for a shandy.

There are older paths from Thirlspot that initially go farther north, to the upper reaches of Fisher Gill or over Brown Crag, but they are obviously very little used now that parking facilities elsewhere have improved so much. One of these paths, however, forms part of a longer but very interesting alternative approach to Helvellyn:

8a. Alternative scramble (or footpath) via Fisher Gill

Only a quarter of a mile north of the King's Head Inn there is a turn-off signed to 'Dale Head Post Office, Thirlspot Farm' where there is limited parking. High on the fellside above is a fine waterfall in Fisher Gill, which provides the line of this route. Low down, the water of Fisher Gill is caught by an aqueduct traversing the fellside, which carries it to Thirlmere. Consequently the stream is only a trickle in its early stages but higher up there is plenty of water and the gill scenery is most spectacular and interesting.

Having parked, turn right in front of the cottages to climb a stile, then go left over another stile and into a stand of larches – many of which lie on the ground having been blown down by gales. There is scrambling up the largely dry stream-bed but it is probably better to bear right a little to a footbridge crossing the aqueduct and then head back towards the now lively stream. This comes down two cascades, which are easily passed, but above these there is a rocky gateway that provides a more entertaining few feet. A waterfall with a jammed boulder is not feasible but the rocks on its right quite easy. They lead unfortunately to a ravine which would need waders to negotiate, so you must leave the gill on the right – but do scramble back to it as soon as possible for the next bit is one of the best. The stream pours down a twisting rock channel and you may follow its course until you emerge underneath a footbridge that links Thirlspot with Stanah Gill and the Sticks Pass.

The forest is now behind and the next section of the gill looks easy but isn't, so go up the left bank with fine views of the upper falls. It is easy to regain the gill just above a holly and another good section follows until further progress is again stopped by a cascade. It is probably as well to give up thoughts of scrambling any farther and go up either side of the gill to view the spectacular upper falls where the water shoots out at one point over vertical crags. Above these the stream runs through a much gentler valley and can be left for the footpath on the right bank. Although this soon disappears, a short climb across the moor towards the rocks of Brown Crag up on the right will soon disclose a fairly faint but cairned path that leads steadily to the summit of Whiteside. Helvellyn Lower Man and the main summit are then soon attained. I do emphasise that there is no need to get involved in any actual scrambling in the bed of Fisher Gill if one chooses not to and the sketchy paths up its sides give excellent places from which to view the very fine gill scenery.

9. Other possible gill scrambles in the area

Stanah Gill

The edge of this gill is the line taken by the Sticks Pass over to Ullswater and the easy scramble up Stanah Gill itself could provide a more entertaining way for part of the distance.

Mill Gill and Beckthorns Gill

Mill Gill is to the left of Castle Rock of Triermain when viewed from the road. I now believe that on my own initial explorations here I went up the wrong gill, which is why I wrote that it was of little interest. I have not had the opportunity to rectify this, but I believe that it is in fact well worth a visit.

Beckthorns Gill is reputedly quite good, though it has a difficult pitch, but there are access difficulties and I have not felt bold enough to face them, so cannot comment.

Sandbeds Gill

This is farther north again and is the very deep-cut gash directly above the southern end of Bram Crag Quarry. There is handy parking space where a track has been fenced off, but this gill is also probably best avoided, as, in any other than drought conditions, it be desperately difficult. The last pitch is definitely the hardest and it is a long way back to the bottom of the gully to escape. For very competent rock-climbers it could be something of a lark, but everybody else should keep away from it. I felt exhilarated but happy to escape unscathed when I climbed it under fairly wet conditions.

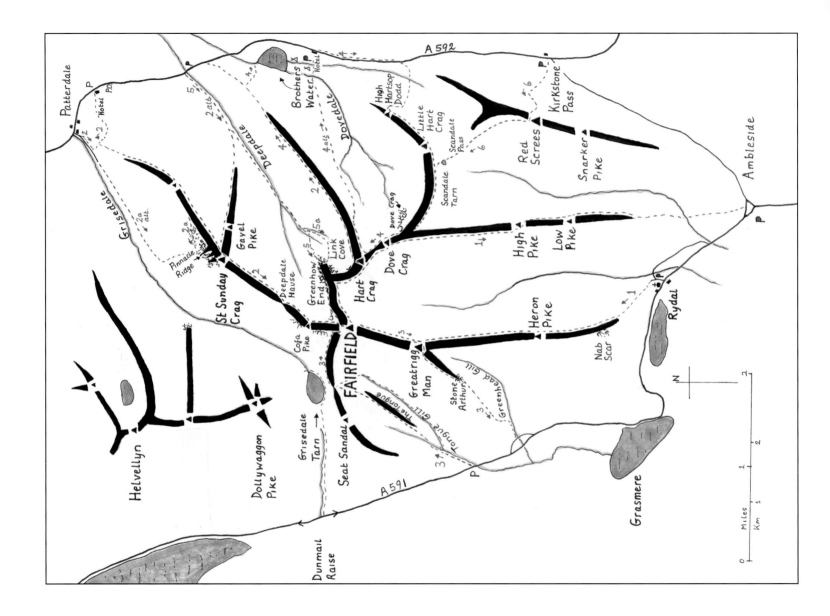

THE FAIRFIELD GROUP

	Approximate Time	Star Rating	Assessment of Difficulty
1. The Fairfield Horseshoe: Nab Scar, Greatrigg, Fairfield; return via Low Pike	5–6 hours	**	—
2. The Fairfield Horseshoe from Patterdale or Deepdale End	5–6 hours	***	—
2a. Alternative scramble on Pinnacle Ridge of St Sunday Crag	add 11/2 hours	***	3
3. Fairfield via Tongue Ghyll and Grisedale Tarn	4 hours	*	—
4. Round of Dovedale over Dove Crag	4 hours	*	—
5. Fairfield from Deepdale via Greenhow End	4–6 hours	***	—
5a. Alternative scrambles: Link Cove Gill and beyond	add 1 hour	***	2–3
6. Traverse of Fairfield via Red Screes (Kirkstone Pass) and the Scandale Pass	4–6 hours	*	—

THE FAIRFIELD GROUP

The Lake District excels in 'horseshoe' walks or 'rounds' where the fell-walker can scale one or a series of peaks by traversing the ridge up one side of a valley and returning along the other, more or less to the original starting point. The summit of Fairfield is the highest point of four or five such walks, not to mention the traverses up a ridge of one valley and down the ridge of the opposing one. With easy accessibility, and situated right in the heart of the National Park, it is understandable why Fairfield is so popular. The highest points of land in this group, which are separated from Helvellyn by the deep and wild trench of Grisedale and from the High Street group by the Kirkstone Pass, are Greatrigg Man, Fairfield, St Sunday Crag, Dove Crag, Hart Crag and Red Screes.

As often occurs in the Lake District, the eastern and south-eastern flanks of these mountains are steeper, wilder, more interesting – though to some people more fearsome – than is suggested by their grassy slopes in other directions. Dove Crag (the cliff, not the innocuous summit rocks) and Hutaple Crag at the head of Deepdale, are tremendous precipices and Dove Crag in particular has some of the most extreme high-standard rock-climbing in the Lake District. For many people the pleasure felt in attaining the summit plateau of Fairfield is greatly enhanced by enough deviation from the route to gaze either down or across these mighty crags.

Once while rock-climbing on Hutaple Crag I made the mistake of thinking that I could easily rescue a sheep, which was trapped on a high ledge. I descended from the summit rocks to get to it, fortunately having enough sense to belay a climbing rope above me. When I reached the ledge where the emaciated sheep was standing it showed no sign of appreciation for its approaching rescue – in fact quite the reverse. It proceeded to rush madly from the prospect of disaster at one end of the ledge towards a similar disaster at the opposite end. The poor animal had long before eaten every available blade of grass and it was, as I found when I caught it

by its fleece, as light as a feather, but it nevertheless still evaded me several times. Had it not been for the rope I might easily have hurtled to the death that the sheep had avoided for so long. Eventually I grabbed it and hung on to the greasy fleece while the animal kicked and struggled and nearly had me over the edge of the cliff. Then with a mighty heave I got it on to a higher ledge from which escape was possible – and the sheep promptly seized this opportunity. The incident left me trembling with the nearness of my own disaster, while the sheep munched voraciously on the higher ledges. I'll certainly never try a sheep rescue on my own again and I have since learned that most farmers simply don't bother, as it's too risky to attempt to rescue cragfast sheep.

To get on with our walks, let's start with the one which is probably the most popular in the area, the Fairfield Horseshoe.

1. The Fairfield Horseshoe: Nab Scar, Greatrigg, Fairfield; return via Low Pike

The traverse of the two southern ridges of Fairfield, which enclose Rydal Beck, gives five or six hours of enjoyable high-level tramping and if the weather is good there should be some marvellous views.

By starting up the westerly ridge it means that you gain height quickly up Nab Scar. If starting from Ambleside, shadow the A591 going north then take the track just beyond Scandale Bridge leading through Rydal Park to Rydal Hall and Wordsworth's former home, Rydal Mount. The path up Nab Scar then climbs steeply on to the main ridge. Personally I am inclined to seek a car parking spot at Rydal and immediately head off up Nab Scar, leaving contemplation of the sylvan beauties of Rydal Park for the return part of the walk.

Wherever you start, Nab Scar, once attained, reveals splendid pastoral views southwards over Rydal Water and Grasmere and down to Windermere. Thereafter the way is obvious, even if the mist comes down, over Heron Pike, Greatrigg and so to the summit of Fairfield. The plateau itself can be a little confusing in mist; for instance there are four stone shelters and the map and compass may be necessary to ensure that the correct line is taken. However, given clear visibility, the very extensive views northwards to the eastern crags and ridges of Helvellyn and then eastwards over Cofa Pike to St Sunday Crag, then down the great valley of Deepdale, are really grand and are often a great surprise to a first-time visitor.

The way to go is then south-east, towards Hart Crag, but sadly the popularity of the walk means that the path along this section is more of a bridle-path. Before reaching Hart Crag there is a short descent to the hause at the head of Link Cove and on the left-hand side is yet another crag, which is better seen while you are climbing the opposite slope. The very name Scrubby Crag doesn't sound very attractive and the approaches to it are a little awkward, but for the rock climber it has some splendid climbs named after figures in Nordic legend: Hrothgar, Grendel and Beowulf.

At the top of the slope you will soon be on Hart Crag and a quarter of a mile farther on the gentle summit of Dove Crag. Unless you make an effort, by going from Hart Crag eastwards towards Brotherswater for instance, you will probably be completely unaware of the presence of the great overhanging precipice of Dove Crag itself. From Dove Crag summit it is undulating easy walking due south down the four-mile long spine of the ridge, crossing High Pike and then Low Pike, and so either back to Ambleside or Rydal. Of course, if you are a really fit fell-runner, you will complete the horseshoe four hours or so before the walker, but you won't have had much chance to appreciate the views.

2. The Fairfield Horseshoe from Patterdale or Deepdale End

Probably less well-known than the previous route, this walk over Fairfield is possibly the best in the group as it gives continuous views of all the finest eastward-facing cliffs and crags in the Fairfield range. It also follows the line of the two most interesting ridges and is in fact the circuit of the Deepdale skyline.

The most obvious starting point is Patterdale (although parking is not easy there), with a quarter-mile walk up the tarmac road up Grisedale and then the footpath heading south-west up Thornhow End. It is much better nowadays to park directly opposite the Patterdale Hotel, where there is a good car park opposite, or in that immediate vicinity. Not only does this mean that refreshments are often to hand on the return, but there is a signed public footpath round the back of the hotel. This leads generally south-west through a landscape of fine deciduous trees, crosses Hag Beck and contours across grassy pastures to reach the spine of the ridge leading up Thornhow End. It is then a steep climb up this to a ladder stile over the intake wall, after which the normal path avoids the line of the public footpath and instead cuts across the flank of

Birks to reach a broad and sometimes boggy hause. From here an obvious path leads up the broad whaleback of St Sunday Crag.

A line of crags on the north-west flank of St Sunday Crag is shown very clearly on local maps, but you will not be aware of these crags as you pace the ridge above. In fact the crags can only be seen to good advantage from Dollywaggon Pike or similar places on the east face of Helvellyn, but hidden away amongst all the rubble of these crumbling rocks lies a really enjoyable scrambling climb called Pinnacle Ridge, to which we'll return later.

An alternative start to this walk could be from Deepdale Bridge, about a mile south of Patterdale. It is not widely known and it avoids the parking problems of Patterdale. It is also more convenient for the return and is a little shorter. Add to these considerations some very fine views up and down Deepdale and across to the High Street fells and you may wonder why more people don't choose this way. While busily selling this approach my innate honesty forces me to admit that it can be a bit boggy when dodging the feeders of Coldcove Gill, before you are able to get on to the firmer ground. However, such considerations are only for wimps, not for robust fell-walkers like you and me.

The first objective is Gavel Pike and after a mile walk up Deepdale leave the valley track just south of the beck of Coldcove Gill. A sketchy path heads up besides this – although it soon fades and you carry on uphill and westwards, regardless. You think you are heading for a broad and grassy ridge, but this is a delusion, as the ground becomes steadily rockier and steeper. Somewhat to your surprise, you arrive on Lord's Seat and there is then a little hause to cross connecting you to Gavel Pike. Once you've arrived there and been delighted by the northern and eastern panorama, you have only a couple of hundred feet farther to the highest point on St Sunday Crag and the equally fine views across Grisedale to Helvellyn and its wild eastern combes.

Having arrived at the summit of St Sunday Crag by whichever route you choose, continue on the good path, down the narrowing ridge to the south-west, to Deepdale Hause linking St Sunday Crag with Cofa Pike and Fairfield. You will surely be aware of mounting excitement as the dramatic views unfold, particularly ahead to Fairfield and Grisedale Tarn and down Deepdale. The sharp little peak of Cofa Pike suddenly rears up as an obstacle to be overcome,

like a policeman barring the route, but you climb up over his helmet and find yourself toiling up a last slope of scree and stones on to Fairfield's summit for a well-deserved rest.

The way is then south-east, descending to the hause at the head of Link Cove, separating Ryedale to the south from Deepdale to the north, then climbing a little to the top of Hart Crag. This same ground, from the summit of Fairfield to Hart Crag, is also covered on the 'original' Fairfield Horseshoe; on this occasion, however, instead of continuing over Dove Crag swing north-east and descend a bouldery ridge until it levels off. With only a slight diversion from the path, the great overhanging cliffs of Dove Crag become much more visible. Also more clearly seen from that point is the commodious cave at the top of the crag, well above the rock-climbing difficulties, that provides a dry shelter for those fell-walkers and climbers who are strong enough to carry up sufficient gear. I myself had planned for years to make use of the cave for a night's sleep as part of a trans-Lakeland walk. The trans-Lakeland walk has never become a reality for me, but I have spent the night there with my then very young son and his friend. I forgot the cooker, so I was in trouble. Whatever it is that has gone wrong, in my family it is always my fault. What's new?

From then on the descent is straightforwardly down the three miles of ridge that separate Dovedale from Deepdale, with many a backward glance at the splendid scenery. If you started at Deepdale Bridge the end of your walk is very near; if from the Patterdale Hotel you have a little road walking to complete your day.

2a. Alternative scramble on Pinnacle Ridge of St Sunday Crag

If, instead of climbing the last steep part of this walk towards the summit of St Sunday Crag, you traverse just below the line of crags on the north-west shoulder of the mountain, you may enjoy a splendid variation to a great day. Pinnacle Ridge connects together various lumps of rock in a fairly continuous line and has two sections on it that are graded 'Difficult' by the rock-climber. For the fell-walker with rock-climbing or reasonably extensive scrambling experience, this route really is a 'must'. On a first visit it isn't particularly easy to locate, but it is worth remembering that it is well towards the left-hand end of the line of crags, with the first deep-cut gully on its right and a distinctive finger of rock pointing out from the ridge rather like a gun barrel. A cairn on a shoulder and a little tree are about

Right: From Gavel Pike to Ullswater and Place Fell.
Overleaf left: Deepdale and Hutaple Crag from Fairfield.
Overleaf right: Cofa Pike and St Sunday Crag from Fairfield.

thirty yards to the left of the correct line as one looks upwards. I have also found that, looking downwards into Grisedale, it is almost directly above the imagined continuation of a very old, collapsed, stone wall running uphill towards you. Fortunately, it is gaining in popularity and so the track to its foot is becoming clearer as each succeeding year goes by. (Pinnacle Ridge can, of course, be approached from below Grisedale, but care in picking the right line up grassy zigzags from Elmhow End is advised, or you will have the horrors of the steep screes to negotiate. One good point, however, is that the 'gun-barrel' can more clearly be seen from this approach.)

Once you have located it you will not need a detailed description; simply climb the most interesting and continuous rock. You can, if you must, scrabble up the earthy gully to the left of the ridge, but if you do that you might as well not have bothered to find it in the first place. As you clamber up the final rocks the summit of St Sunday Crag is only a couple of hundred yards away. I have enjoyed this so much that on one occasion I climbed it from below, then climbed down it, then climbed back up it again.

I once went with a party of friends to do this route and, because it was misty and freezing hard when we left Patterdale, we walked up Grisedale instead of the ridge, failed to find the grassy zigzags way and had to toil up the steep slopes for what seemed hours. We did the scramble all right, but it was icy in places and by the time we reached the summit plateau it was snowing hard. The rest of us decided that we'd had enough for the day and retreated for a warm brew-up in Patterdale. One of our friends, however, decided that he hadn't had enough exercise and that he was going to continue over to Grisedale Tarn, up Dollywaggon Pike and over Helvellyn. He pronounced that he would be in Kendal by about 5 p.m. but even with all his extensive Alpine and Himalayan experience behind him he did not arrive until after 8 p.m. We were not quite sure whether or not to believe him when he admitted to having been lost – but only for a few minutes(!) – in a complete whiteout on Helvellyn.

3. Fairfield via Tongue Ghyll and Grisedale Tarn

Another attractive round, and the shortest, starts a mile north of Grasmere village. Do not be misled by a sign at the bottom of Tongue Ghyll on the main road, which says 'Helvellyn' but does not mention Fairfield; both are attainable via Grisedale Tarn. If you take the well-used and, I must admit, much improved track that follows the course of the main stream rushing down Tongue Ghyll you will certainly get to Grisedale Tarn, but you will have taken the most obvious and perhaps the least interesting way. Better to leave the main stream just after the second gate and take the left-hand stream branch instead, so that you may follow the old packhorse road. The initial steep climb is soon over, leads over a shoulder on to the flank of Seat Sandal and then traverses across the fell at a more comfortable angle and with just a short climb to reach Grisedale Tarn.

For a third alternative an energetic walker could approach Grisedale Tarn by taking the curving south-west ridge to the unjustly neglected summit of Seat Sandal, which gives good views down Grisedale, before descending a little way to Grisedale Hause. Personally I prefer to pick a line up the Great Tongue, the grassy spur between the packhorse road and the stream up Tongue Ghyll, which has the attraction of having no path at all.

Having arrived at Grisedale Tarn, the route to take up the west ridge of Fairfield is well-tracked and obvious enough and in normal weather is just a straightforward slog uphill. However, in windy or icy conditions it can seem very exposed, particularly in descent, and it is at times and in places such as this that the inadequacies of many walkers' equipment and clothing become apparent. Incidentally, crampons that weigh so very little indeed can be an extremely useful addition to an ice-axe on ground like this when it is icy.

I recall doing this walk one winter's day and meeting some lads who were apparently descending Tongue Ghyll. However, when I reached the party, one of them was totally wrapped up in a plastic bag and lying on the ground. The others greeted me with the question 'Are you the Mountain Rescue?' I told them that I wasn't, which was evidently a disappointment, but asked them why they were there. 'Well, our friend here was in a bad way,' was the reply. I asked whether he was injured or anything like that. 'No!' piped up the voice of the youth in the plastic bag, sticking his head out. 'I felt cold and tired, slipping about up there, coming down from Fairfield so we decided we'd have to wait for me to be rescued.' 'Are you cold now?' I asked. 'Oh no, I'm quite warm now,' was the answer. 'Then my advice to you is that you get up out of that bag and walk down to the valley,' I said. 'If the Mountain Rescue has no more urgent case than you, you'll probably meet the team on the way up.'

Such counsel of self-help seemed to cause consternation. They looked at me in open amazement as I shouldered my sack and pressed on uphill.

Once on the summit plateau, the way is due south, descending gently and then rising slightly on the well-defined ridge to Greatrigg Man and eventually down the stony ridge on the south side. Leave the main ridge there and descend south-west to Stone Arthur, after which the quickest way is a steep and rather jarring descent down the footpath which meets the bottom of Greenhead Gill and so to the north side of Grasmere village.

Incidentally there is only a very sketchy footpath down the upper part of Greenhead Gill, but I have twice in the past had excellent ski-runs from Fairfield via Greatrigg down the slopes of this gill and almost to the road. Will we ever see snow lasting long enough to do this in future?

A longer, but less exhausting descent can be made by going south on the main ridge as far as the knobble of Heron Pike and then heading west downhill towards Greenhead Gill. With care, it should be easy to pick up the upper part of the well-used footpath that leads northwards from Alcock Tarn into Greenhead Gill and so to the A591 just north of the turn-offs into Grasmere.

4. Round of Dovedale over Dove Crag

The map should show this possibility clearly enough: High Hartsop Dodd, Little Hart Crag, Black Brow, Dove Crag and then down the north east ridge to Bridgend. When you arrive there is usually adequate parking near the Brotherswater Hotel.

The problem is getting on to the well defined ridge of High Hartsop Dodd because the footpaths in the valley bottom are all on private land and the owners actively discourage any approach. The answer is to walk up the Kirkstone Pass road, cross the Caiston Beck at any convenient point and make a rising traverse to get on to the obvious ridge to High Hartsop Dodd. Then it is straightforwardly upwards and westwards to pick up the main path that climbs from the Scandale Pass. This path then follows the watershed over the summit of Dove Crag on to Hart Crag and so north-east down the ridge between Deepdale and Dovedale. Alternatively you can finish down the path that eventually winds through the lovely woods of Dovedale.

If you stay on the ridge, beware the temptation to descend to the east too soon. The slopes above the south end of Brotherswater are desperate indeed, having loose scree, rocks, tree branches and brambles. It is the sort of place where an ankle can easily be broken and it is much better to stay on the ridge until beyond the north end of Brotherswater where a reasonable path via a ladder-stile heads down through bracken and trees to the car park just off the road.

4a. Fairfield from Raise Beck

This is a straightforward ascent starting from the main A591 (Grasmere–Keswick) road at Dunmail Raise and going directly up the right-hand side of Raise Beck. It is a steady climb and the fine view of Grisedale Tarn is a welcome relief, before heading up the west ridge of Fairfield to the top. Obviously this route to the tarn gives the most direct connection with Patterdale, and the stony path leads underneath Tarn Crag, below the east face coves of Helvellyn, and down to the head of Ullswater. It hardly ranks as one of the best walks in the Lake District, and I am not counting it as such, but it is a useful and speedy way to better things.

5. Fairfield from Deepdale via Greenhow End

The Ullswater end of Deepdale is very attractive, with its delicate larches and other trees set in green pastures, all surrounded by the lower slopes of the high fells. There is usually good parking at the end of Deepdale but many people seem to have mixed feelings about the walk up Deepdale itself, which is about three miles long. Indeed, I know some who feel that the only suitable frame of mind for going up there is that induced by the old Army command of 'switch off brains, switch on feet'. On a cold winter's day when the sun's rays have difficulty penetrating to the valley bottom I can perhaps share the sentiment, but at most other seasons it is a very pleasant walk and well worth the effort, for you are soon amidst fine rock scenery and rushing waters.

The rocky bulk of Greenhow End, which terminates the long spur from Fairfield and which has Hutaple Crag on one side and Scrubby Crag on the other, above Link Cove, rises steeply ahead. The main path, which has stayed close to the course of the beck, begins to rise away from it, heading for Deepdale Hause. A less well-defined path, however, winds up into Link Cove through an area of drumlins. This is the track to follow.

A gully splits the steep rocks of Greenhow End into two main sections and a cairned path leads up a vaguely defined rake to the left of the left-hand section

Looking up Deepdale to Greenhow End, Hutaple Crag and Fairfield.

where the angle is easier. This zigzags to the top of the buttress. A quite narrow and rocky ridge follows, giving exhilarating walking, overlooking the great cliffs of Hutaple and on to Fairfield's summit. A worthy return would, of course, be along either of the retaining ridges. I do not suggest that this route is better, say, than the Deepdale skyline route already described, but it does get you right into the heart of that scenery which is so wild, rugged and eye-catching when it is seen from the heights above. Don't let anybody else's ideas about the three-mile approach put you off!

5a. Alternative scrambles: Link Cove Gill and beyond

To make the expedition to Fairfield even more worth while here is one of the very best scrambles to be found in the Lake District. The scenery is most attractive and the route is an excellent and entertaining one for competent and experienced scramblers. Reasonably dry conditions will be found best for tackling this course and a short rope will prove very useful.

Link Cove Gill contains the left-hand of the two streams that flow down from Link Cove and it is the more defined. Start up the slabs on the left-hand side of the initial waterslide and climb up to the ravine above, under trees. A short waterfall splashes into a pool but there is obviously a way up the right-hand side of the cascade – if you can reach it. To avoid wet feet move delicately across holds on the right wall of the pool just above water level, then scramble up to easier ground. Ahead is a much more intimidating cascade and little persuasion will be needed to transfer to the rocky rib above the right edge of the ravine.

Incidentally, non-scramblers will find this rib a fairly easy way and one that will provide them with good views of the antics in the gill.

At the top of the long waterfall care is needed for an exposed step down. A little traverse then leads back into the gill and another, deeper pool and cascade await. A ledge for feet on the left wall and good handholds make a step down feasible to avoid a wetting. Climb a groove on the left of the watercourse to emerge into an amphitheatre, with sloping slabby sides which steepen towards the top. Easy climbing leads up the lower half heading leftwards. An exposed finish just to the left of the cascade looks – and is – feasible, but intimidating. Most scramblers will prefer to go further left and will be able to surmount a little wall with direct aid from a short rope. This may be thrown over the trunk of a stout tree just above the wall and it will prove much more reliable than a handful of heather roots. Above the tree a little traverse leads back to the gill above the cascade. There are still waterfalls and fine slabs ahead and the stream bed may be followed farther for quite some distance as the ravine merges into the hillside.

The steeper rock of Greenhow End will be very apparent on the right so strike up towards it. A cairned path heads up a grassy rake to the right, reaches a shoulder then zigzags back left. This provides the normal walking way up. One may, however, find a scramble way up the rocks to the left of the rake. It is much easier than in the gill below and it is really a matter of simply finding the best rock for interesting upward progress. One shortly emerges on the walkers' route nearer the top of the buttress.

6. Traverse of Fairfield via Red Screes (Kirkstone Pass) and the Scandale Pass

As a starting and finishing point for walkers on the Fairfield group, there are many better places than the top of the Kirkstone Pass. It is, however, a good place to start a traverse of the main peaks, with the aim of finishing in Grasmere or Ambleside – so long of course as your transport is organised.

The climb up the rubble of the Red Screes by sketchy paths is not quite so awful as it looks and, once on the plateau above, you join the long ridge path coming up from Ambleside via Snarker Pike. It is then gently downhill north-westwards over open moorland to the watershed of the Scandale Pass. Finding a tiny tarn near the crossing point is a relief and a comfort if the weather has turned misty, because the watershed is only gently defined. It is then a steady climb over grassy moorland to a very prominent cairn – a really big one like Robinson's cairn on Pillar, or like a mini-Thornthwaite Beacon – which is large enough to be marked on most maps. Continue over Dove Crag's summit and on to Hart Crag and Fairfield. You then have a choice of scenic descent routes, down the west ridge of Fairfield to Grisedale Tarn, then Tongue Ghyll or Raise Beck. Alternatively you may descend to Rydal or Grasmere from the ridge to and beyond Greatrigg Man. As you descend to the gentle smoke rising from the hearths of Rydal or Grasmere you may reflect on yet another fine day's walking on these incomparable hills. No wonder some of our greatest poets chose to live in such splendid surroundings.

Helvellyn seen beyond Cofa Pike, from Fairfield.

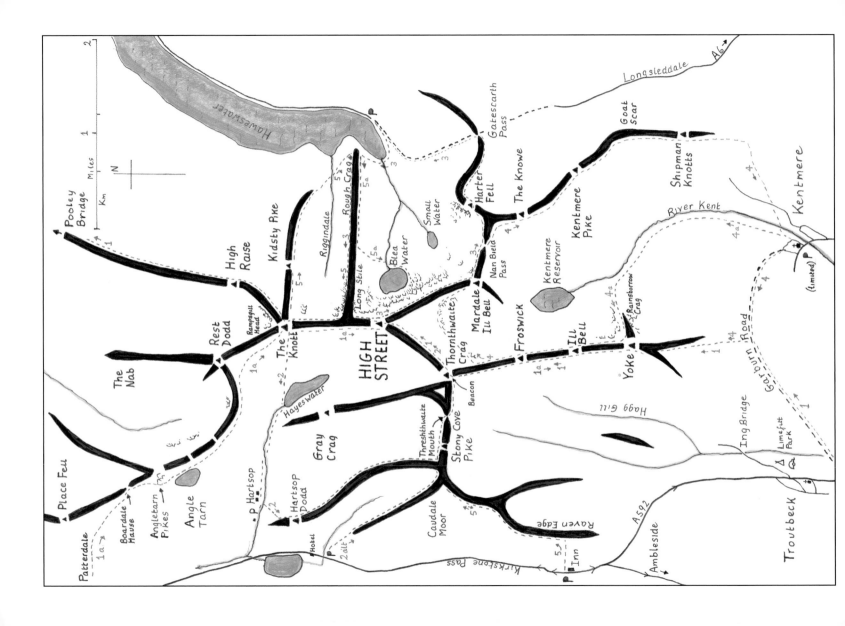

HIGH STREET, MARDALE and KENTMERE

	Approximate Time	Star Rating	Assessment of Difficulty
1. The Traverse of High Street: Troutbeck to Pooley Bridge	5–7 hours	**	—
1a. Alternative shorter version: traverse of High Street from Patterdale to Troutbeck	4–6 hours	**	—
2. High Street from Hartsop via Stoney Cove Pike, Thornthwaite Beacon, and The Knott	4–5 hours	*	—
3. High Street and Harter Fell from Haweswater	5–6 hours	***	—
4. The Kentmere Round	6–7 hours	***	—
4a. Alternative scramble on Rainsborrow Crag	add 1 hour	*	2
5. High Street, Kidsty Pike, Haweswater and Rough Crag; start and finish at the Kirkstone Pass	7–8 hours	**	—
5a. Alternative scramble in Blea Water Crag Gill	add 1–2 hours	**	2

HIGH STREET, MARDALE and KENTMERE

1. The Traverse of High Street: Troutbeck to Pooley Bridge

High Street used to be called Racecourse Hill and the actual summit area is still marked as such on the O.S. 1:25000 maps. For years, until 1835, it was the meeting place for shepherds from the surrounding valleys to exchange strayed sheep. They also raced horses along the plateau, with the usual wagers and carousing that always accompany such jolly outings. Long before then the Romans also used the hill as a highway for their marching legionaries and the present name reminds us that we were once an outpost for their Empire. In times when the valleys of England were thick with woods and marshes, when the ancient 'forests' really were afforested, the existence of such a high ridge, in an almost direct line, probably meant both safety and speed.

You may prefer to climb up on to the more dramatic southern fells when doing this longer version of the traverse and get the hard work over. Later in the day, after Loadpot Hill, it will all be downhill and you can cruise comfortably in the confident assumption that your ever-patient partner will either be waiting for you or will have left the car. . . . Beware of suggestions that Sharrow Bay is a good place to rendezvous or you may have a very well-fed partner and a large bill as well!

From Troutbeck you must first get up to the ridge. The Romans did it by marching up Hagg Gill and thus avoided some of the best bits of the walk. They weren't, however, interested in the mountain scenery so don't follow in their footsteps. Instead, just before the Kirkstone Pass road, coming from the south, crosses Trout Beck at Church Bridge, find the stony track on the right, a couple of hundred paces south of the church. This becomes the Garburn 'road' linking Troutbeck and Kentmere. Although rough in parts, it enables you to walk fairly painlessly up to the top of the pass.

The ridge may also be reached a little farther north by walking from Ing Bridge up a grassy spur with a path that peters out high on the fell. Sadly there are parking problems in this area if you intend to leave a car and it will be easier nearer to the caravan site at Limefitt Park. Nipping over a stile gives access to the fellside and then a short climb enables you to join the Garburn road easily.

At the top of the pass the ridge is broad, open and rather featureless, but a good path rapidly leads northwards and in a mile and a half of easy walking you reach the first summit of Yoke. From then on the ridge sharpens. There are views down into Kentmere as you peer over the rocky summit of Ill Bell and along the crest of the ridge towards Froswick, the next objective, which is about a mile away. Beyond Froswick you should be able to see the striking obelisk of Thornthwaite Beacon.

I was walking this ridge one spring day when I found a large parcel. Actually there were three of us and we all spotted the object, but I won the race to reach it first. It was orange in colour and appeared to be a cagoule, but then we realised that it was in fact a tent. This was a bit of a puzzle for the only signs of any other recent human passage were the tyre-marks of a motorbike. Apart from the noise they make, which on the open footpaths of the high Lakeland fells is an affront to everybody else, their tyres cause more damage in half an hour than boots do in months. We worked ourselves into a state of high indignation over the unknown motorcyclist, while the tent – which we thought must have dropped off the back of the bike – was shoved into my rucksack. Somebody would be looking for it, we thought, and if it were a motorcyclist we would let him sweat it out a bit and be sure he knew what we thought before returning it. Sure enough, when we tramped up the slope from Froswick to Thornthwaite Beacon we saw a young chap, looking very agitated, scratching his head and looking at his map. Eventually he asked us if we had seen anything so we asked him what he was looking for and it was the tent all right. It was clear that he wasn't the motorcyclist and so I handed it over very willingly, for it was quite heavy. How anybody's load could be so suddenly lightened by so much without the owner noticing for so long is still a mystery to me.

Thornthwaite Beacon, atop Thornthwaite Crags, is a fine viewpoint, particularly back along the Froswick–Ill Bell ridge, away to the farthest misty reaches of Windermere and across the head of Hayeswater Gill to the long whaleback hump of High Street itself. With its stone wall turning along its crest it doesn't look very exciting, but it is deceptive, for from there you are only aware of the gentler contours. Tramp up towards the triangulation point on the highest ground, however, and then head away a little eastwards from the path and you will discover that this is no inferior mountain. Its east face, looking down to Haweswater, is almost as dramatic as the east face of Helvellyn. The splendid ridge of Long Stile–Rough Crag separates two great combes. The one on the north (left) is Riggindale, with Kidsty Pike standing proudly above it. The combe on the right (north) contains the beautifully shaped tarn of Blea Water. If, however, you have stayed on the line of the Roman road on this part of the walk, you will see none of this grandeur unless you look back on reaching the Straits of Riggindale. There the path forks leftwards towards the lump of The Knott or rightwards towards the fine eminence of Kidsty Pike. The latter is a good spot for a sandwich overlooking Haweswater.

Now return to the path running above the cliffs of Rampsgill Head and press on to reach High Raise, which is really only a swelling on the ridge. The steep, grassy slopes below on the left, and even more so those of The Nab on the other side of Rampsgill, are deer forest and small herds may often be spotted on the fellside. Both roe deer and red deer, which seemed for so long to be restricted to just a few areas in the Lake District, seem to be staging a comeback. This area around Martindale was thought to be one of the last remaining places for them in Lakeland but we have regularly had them in the gardens even in Grasmere in the last few winters. There, the revival has been so dramatic that some have had to be culled.

It is fast and easy walking, still along the line of the old Roman road, though there is little enough evidence of it nowadays. Just after Red Crag a footpath runs down into Fusedale, but you must stay on the high land. Wether Hill and Loadpot Hill are soon left behind. The light glints on Ullswater ahead, largely hidden by the Martindale Fells so far, and you can whistle cheerfully as you cruise along downhill to journey's end at Pooley Bridge.

1a. Alternative shorter version: traverse of High Street from Patterdale to Troutbeck

This is possibly a better walk – except for purists – because it incorporates all the most scenically interesting sections and is shorter.

Just north of the Patterdale Hotel a track crosses the valley floor, goes over the Goldrill Beck, through some outbuildings and so on to the steep side of Place Fell.

Long Stile ridge rising to High Street; Harter Fell beyond.

The path you need starts across the steep slope, heading for Boardale Hause, but swings south just before it reaches it and makes a way across moorland – with a good view at one point down to Brotherswater in Patterdale. The rocky little summits of Angle Tarn Pikes are ahead and the path unsportingly traverses under them and then down, to skirt Angle Tarn itself. Beware of stopping for lunch if there are sheep about, for in winter particularly they have been known to practically trample walkers underfoot in their eagerness to steal sandwiches and other morsels of food. (I am quite serious about this!)

The usually boggy bit that follows is more interesting if you get close to the rocks of Prison Crag, which gives fine views towards Caudale Head. Unfortunately it is then quite a trudge up to the lump of The Knott.

I was once sitting behind the wall on the The Knott drinking the last drop of coffee in the flask and thinking of descent, for it was very misty and much worse higher up. As I was just about to leave I realised that a party of a dozen or so fell-walkers were all dithering about on the slopes below. I was going in that direction anyway and as I approached they asked me the name of the sheet of water that could dimly be seen down below and which was, of course, Hayeswater. They were greatly surprised and had in fact been well and truly lost, thinking that they were descending to Troutbeck in the opposite direction. They brightened up when they realised exactly where they were and began to tramp back up towards High Street. I never heard any more of them, so I assumed that they all returned home safely.

From The Knott you have a fine view of the cliffs of Rampsgill Head and High Raise and the path from the northern part of the old Roman road, which you are missing out, joins your path at the Straits of Riggindale. From then on, particularly if you stay close to the eastern edge of High Street, even after you have passed the O.S. pillar on the summit, you will get splendid views down Rough Crag to Mardale, Blea Water and Haweswater. In mist, however, stay alongside the wall and when it ends swing round towards the fine cairn of Thornthwaite Beacon. The Romans descended from Thornthwaite Crags down the slope of the fell into Hagg Gill and you also can walk down the line that they took, into the valley and so back to Troutbeck, if you have had enough of the high ground. It is much better, however, to stay on the ridge, and it doesn't feel so far either. So go over Froswick and Ill Bell to Yoke and then follow the moortop to the Garburn 'road', Your finishing point, and hopefully your transport, should be just down the hill in Troutbeck.

2. High Street from Hartsop via Stony Cove Pike, Thornthwaite Beacon and The Knott

The possibilities of these fine fells have by no means been exhausted after the traverse of High Street. This is a shorter day, but it is a round, with its advantages, and it takes in nearly all the best bits of mountain scenery on this side of the main High Street ridge.

There is a choice as to which way to go up to Stony Cove Pike from or near Hartsop village, as the ridges up Caudale Moor and Hartsop Dodd run parallel to each other and link up at Stony Cove Pike. Both of them are steep. Hartsop Dodd is the fine prow that juts down towards Ullswater and it is very prominent while travelling from Patterdale towards Kirkstone.

If opting for the direct route up Hartsop Dodd it is best to park at the east end of Hartsop village, as a bridge and good path from there cross Pasture Beck and lead straight up the nose of the Dodd. Then an almost continuous wall leads to Stony Cove Pike.

Alternatively, for a change, there is a useful large lay-by at Caudale Bridge, just south of the Brotherswater Inn. From here a path leads fairly steeply uphill to the south-east to reach some old mine workings. Then it climbs interestingly along a sharper ridge (Rough Edge) to reach the much more level Caudale Moor. Stony Cove Pike is then near at hand. It is worth bearing in mind that this is not an isolated viewpoint, being merely a slightly more prominent pile of rocks in a rocky area, so that in mist it can be difficult to be sure that you have reached it. However, when clear, you can look over Hagg Gill to the shapely summits of Ill Bell and Froswick, which are actually a little lower in height. There is also a fine view of the gentler side of the High Street ridge, which is the next objective, across the upper reaches of Hayeswater Gill.

It is necessary to descend into the gap of the Threshwaite Mouth, which is a steep and rocky descent and an equally steep climb up the eroded slope opposite. In winter I have known the upward slope to be negotiable only with an ice-axe for balance and crampons for a secure footing because it has been so iced-up. Indeed it is always harder walking up that particular slope than one remembers, but the elegant pillar of the Beacon is not far away. Occasionally, it is not only a fine spot on which to stand and count how many mountains you can identify but, from the amount of orange peel and other litter that some louts leave, it is also an almost irresistible place for lunch.

A mile away, across gentler slopes, lie the 'vast sheep runs' of the High Street and the path that follows the old Roman road leads steadily round and towards them. However, to reach the actual summit you need to head for the line of the wall and follow that. It is a better way, for you are nearer to the splendid east face and so much more likely to be aware of the wild scenery down to Blea Water and Haweswater. The Roman centurions, of course, marched resolutely across the gentle slopes above Haweswater and didn't take a peep down the east face until they reached the Straits of Riggindale. Perhaps the odd defaulter was then tipped over the edge.

It is then only a short distance to The Knott, after which you can plunge down the grassy and sometimes very soggy slope on the path leading to the outflow from Hayeswater. From there it is an obvious, though in places rocky, path down the line of Hayeswater Gill and so back to Hartsop village or to your transport near the Brotherswater Inn.

3. High Street and Harter Fell from Haweswater

This round isn't far in map miles – seven or eight at most, unless you add on a bit by going out to Kidsty Pike or somewhere like that – but this is certainly the best walk in the area.

Your way lies up the dramatic ridge of Rough Crag and High Stile, directly to the top of High Street. The mountain scenery is very fine and the ridge thrusts right into the centre of the splendid east face of High Street and even juts into Haweswater itself.

As you drive up the road on the east side of the reservoir, it is worth while stopping at the long bend, just before Hopgill Beck flows into the lake, and walking for a few minutes up the Old Corpse Road (which is signposted) towards Swindale and Shap. Before the (now drowned) church at Mardale Green was built, the dead of the hamlet were carried on horseback over to Shap for a consecrated burial and, as they left Mardale for ever, they certainly left behind them a most wonderful view of the head of the valley. The loneliness, beauty and grandeur are so outstanding that it is no wonder that eagles keep returning. Fell-walkers of a slightly older vintage than myself (and there aren't that many left now) recall the submerged hamlet with sorrow and nostalgia and whenever the level of the reservoir is low in a year of drought there are always curious folk to be found wandering around the collapsed walls and remains of the village that are revealed. Personally I accept Haweswater as an almost natural phenomenon. Certainly the view from up on the Old Corpse Road is enhanced by the presence of the long arm of the lake lapping round The Rigg. In addition, virtually all your day's walk can be seen ahead of you.

Once you have parked at Mardale Head a well-marked track leads you forward rapidly, but avoid any branches going off to the left up to the Gatescarth Pass or ahead to the Nan Bield Pass. Instead, go to the right, round the head of the reservoir, then follow the path which leads gently to a grassy shoulder above the wooded end of the promontory (The Rigg). The next stretch doubles back and goes up the long ridge of Rough Crag. It is a most enjoyable ascent, firstly just to the left of the ridge (if you stay on the path) and then on its stony crest, with views down one side into Riggindale and down the other to the steep and rocky country which forms a wild cirque above the beautiful pearl-shape of Blea Water. Descend a little to the grassy saddle called Caspel Gate and then go up again, on or around the steeper rocks of Long Stile. With a last exhilarated puff you reach a cairn and you are there. The triangulation pillar on the almost flat summit plateau of High Street is only a few horizontal paces away. The contrast is most striking.

The next objective is the rocky lump of Mardale Ill Bell, which is farther on around the cirque of Blea Water Crag. As usual, a footpath across the sloping moor is the quickest way if you are in a hurry, but you'll miss the best views. Better to skirt the edge of the crags.

If you do reach Mardale Ill Bell in a mist, take a compass bearing and remember that for the next bit – over to the Nan Bield – you are descending across a hillside, not clinging to a ridge.

I have, of course, in the past failed to take my own advice. On one occasion on this walk I missed the path, in snow and mist, followed the broad ridge south down to Lingmell End – expecting to see the Nan Bield Pass at any moment – and not until we got below the mist and could see Kentmere Reservoir literally yards away did we find out just where we were. It was January and nearly dark. The long, long trudge up the hairpins of the Nan Bield and back to Mardale that night will not easily be expunged from my memory. Then we had a three hour drive.

Once you reach the pass, where a solid rock windbreak defies the prevailing south-westerlies, you can, of course, descend past Small Water to Mardale without

Right: The head of Haweswater, looking up Riggindale.
Overleaf left: Haweswater from the Old Corpse Road.
Overleaf right: Haweswater from Harter Fell

more ado. However, press on up the opposite slope, swinging left as the angle eases, to reach the summit of Harter Fell, whose highly individual cairn still bristles with bits of old iron fencing.

The path continues north-east, heading apparently directly for Haweswater and the tendency is to press on eagerly. If, however, you stay blindly on this line you'll either go straight down the big gully that splits the face or go over the rocks that buttress Harter Fell's northern flank. There is a fine view of Mardale from that point and also of Blea Water and High Street, but to descend safely you will need to swing south-east away from the crags and curve downhill and round to the Gatesgarth Pass. All that remains is to walk the zigzags and grassy slopes back to the car park and the end of a memorable walk.

4. The Kentmere Horseshoe

This fine circuit is probably best done in a clockwise direction, keeping the main moorland walking for the return half of the day.

Kentmere is more a hamlet than a village, with narrow, winding lanes and isolated houses, none of which, sadly, is a pub. However, I do recall that we once 'conned' a friend into paying for a splendid farmhouse tea there years ago. That was a feat almost as great as doing the walk itself!

An early start is advisable to be able to park in the only place, between the phone box and the church, then make a start along the road beyond until the track can be seen heading through a cluster of farm buildings and across fields. Kentmere Hall is shortly in view on the left and then a rough track (the Garburn road) leads beyond the confines of the intake fields. On reaching the Garburn Pass the walk really begins, for the fine hills to the west can be seen and at last there is open moor ahead. The path leaves the 'road' as you turn right and some boggy bits are soon left behind when the moor narrows and reaches the first summit of Yoke. For the first time it is then possible to see where you are going. In front is the climb to Ill Bell while down the steep slopes to the right, a long way below, is Kentmere Reservoir. Beyond lie Mardale Ill Bell and the Nan Bield Pass. There is a feeling of exhilaration, for you are on a fine, easy, and airy ridge, with cares forgotten and plenty of energy in hand. Ill Bell is soon left behind and there is a steep descent before another climb up to Froswick. The strange dyke or gully on the flank of The Knowe on the fellside opposite is a curiosity, for it looks as though some giant potato peeler scooped it

out but never finished the job. Ahead lies Thornthwaite Beacon, but just before the last slope up to it, by three old iron fence posts planted close together, veer to the right, heading round the rim of Hall Cove. A narrower footpath winds and curves round above Kentmere and then gently climbs the peaty moor to Mardale Ill Bell.

The flanking descent to the Nan Bield Pass soon follows. While pausing on the pass itself there is an excellent view down upper Kentmere, across the reservoir to Ill Bell and Froswick and, in particular, to the sharp edge of Rainsborrow Crag, buttressing Yoke. You tramped that skyline a few hours ago and would never have suspected the existence of those great rocks.

Ahead is the steep, short, climb up to Harter Fell, its summit cairn bristling with old iron railings. Now the ridge fence is a totally reliable guide and a gentle descent and short pull up again soon lead to Kentmere Pike where the O.S. triangulation point is largely hidden over a wall. Continuing the ridge ahead is a simple matter of following either the wall or the fence where the wall has not survived, going over the peaty ground and then veering rightwards to Kentmere. However, the impression of a dull, broad-backed ridge is greatly changed if you see it from down in the valley of Longsleddale, for the many steep crags on that flank, not seen from the ridge path, contribute greatly to the grandeur of the head of the valley. A slight diversion from the main path to the summit rocks of Goat Scar to see this is well worth while. From there you may survey the wild country to where the Gatescarth Pass crosses from Mardale and look across to the rocks of Buckbarrow Crag. Although it is over forty years since I climbed there, I can still remember a moment of fright when a vital bit of rock came away in my hand. A return to the fence and wall soon leads to the straightforward descent to Kentmere. If you miss a footpath and find yourself on tarmac for a little way it does not matter, for a couple of well-signed stiles point the way over the Kent by a footbridge and so back to the church.

4a. Alternative scramble on Rainsborrow Crag

From the Nan Bield Pass, the edge of the crags running from the summit of Yoke to the valley floor look impressive and this edge provides an interesting variation start to the Kentmere Round. As a rock scramble its interest is restricted to the first twenty or thirty feet, after which it becomes an energetic walk up bilberry ledges. It is, however, a direct, natural line to Yoke, which Harry Griffin first pointed out in one of his books.

The head of Longsleddale seen from Goat Scar.

From the church in Kentmere walk towards Hartrigg Farm up the level valley and on the west (left) side of the River Kent. Farther on there are quarries and some cottages, just before the reservoir. A stream flows down past the cottages and can be used as a way up to the route, which is up the right-hand edge of the crags on the left. The approach to the bottom of the buttress is very steep and the rock doubtful, so it should be avoided, but a grassy terrace runs up to it above the initial bit. A slanting line of weakness in a bold position then leads to a ledge and easier ground. From then on it is airy but very easy scrambling up ledges for quite a long way until the ridge narrows, passes a little pool and then fades into the grassy summit of Yoke.

5. High Street, Kidsty Pike, Haweswater and Rough Crag; start and finish at the Kirkstone Pass

The car park at the head of Mardale is in scenically marvellous country, but it isn't easy to reach. The Kirkstone Pass on the other hand, 1,500 feet above sea level, is much easier to attain. This walk is a challenge, but it enables a strong walker to have a contrived but very good day over virtually all the best ground on the High Street fells. It will be best appreciated when you have some prior knowledge of the area.

There is plenty of parking at the top of Kirkstone Pass, then you have a stiff but short pull up St Raven's Edge, 400 feet higher. The path stays with the wall, which dips and climbs steadily up the open moor, to a little pile of stones that marks the eminence of John Bell's Banner. A little farther and higher and you are on Stony Cove Pike. Then a quick dash down into Threshwaite Mouth and a puff up the other side gets you to Thornthwaite Beacon. It should be much too early for lunch: don't even think about it until you have traversed High Street and walked out to Kidsty Pike. If it is a warm day, however, you may still prefer to continue down the gentle ridge beyond Kidsty Pike to Kidsty Howes and the peaty slope running down to the Riggindale Beck. There you may drink, listen to the lapping of the wavelets at the edge of Haweswater and the croak of the ravens, where once were fields of Mardale Green.

The great spur of Rough Crag is an irresistibly direct way back to the heights, but don't burn up all your energy by going too quickly. The gentle curve of the High Street Plateau is ahead again, just above the steeper slopes of Long Stile, but remember that you still have the return to Thornthwaite Beacon, the descent to Threshwaite Mouth and a climb back up the other side.

When you set foot again on Stony Cove Pike you can really begin to relax, for it is then all downhill to the Kirkstone Pass.

5a. Alternative scramble in Blea Water Crag Gill

The head of Mardale has a lot of interesting-looking rocky ground and Harter Fell has several obvious gullies, which, under winter ice, might give good routes for competent mountaineers. Elsewhere there are possibilities, but they don't quite live up to their promise. The spur that separates Blea Water from Small Water has Piot Crag on its end and a good direct route up Mardale Ill Bell can be achieved by making use of it, preferably by starting near Blea Water. Unfortunately the rock is rather discontinuous for good scrambling and it is only when the thousand-foot wall rising to High Street behind Blea Water is considered that a good way is to be found. Make no mistake: it is a good way, but only for a scrambler with some experience.

Blea Water can be approached from Mardale, of course, or by descending to it from Caspel Gate on the Rough Crag–Long Stile ridge, which enables one to pick out the line on the approach.

Avoid the prominent and deeply cut central gully and go to the left of it where the rim dips a little between High Street and Mardale Ill Bell. Here there is a less obvious watercourse over various rock steps. A deep cleft in the rock immediately above the scree is a bit too awkward and intimidating to start, so go up to the left and then back right to avoid the steepest bit. Attractive scrambling follows up a series of cascades to the foot of a very wide band of steep rock down which the water splashes. In very dry conditions this barrier can be scaled – by those with rock-climbing experience – on the far right where the slabs are bounded by a rock corner; but it is normally advisable for others to keep well to the left and regain the line of the stream a little higher up. More good scrambling follows, with rock ramps at various points enabling height to be gained. There is clean, sound rock in most of the overflow channels, which is useful in evading the cascades. Near the top, as it becomes less steep, a pleasant little rocky ridge on the right of the stream leads on to the open moor where the watercourse fades away into the peat. It is then only a short walk to High Street's top and you can happily let the wind dry off your kit as you stroll over to the summit.

On Rough Crag; Long Stile and High Street ahead.

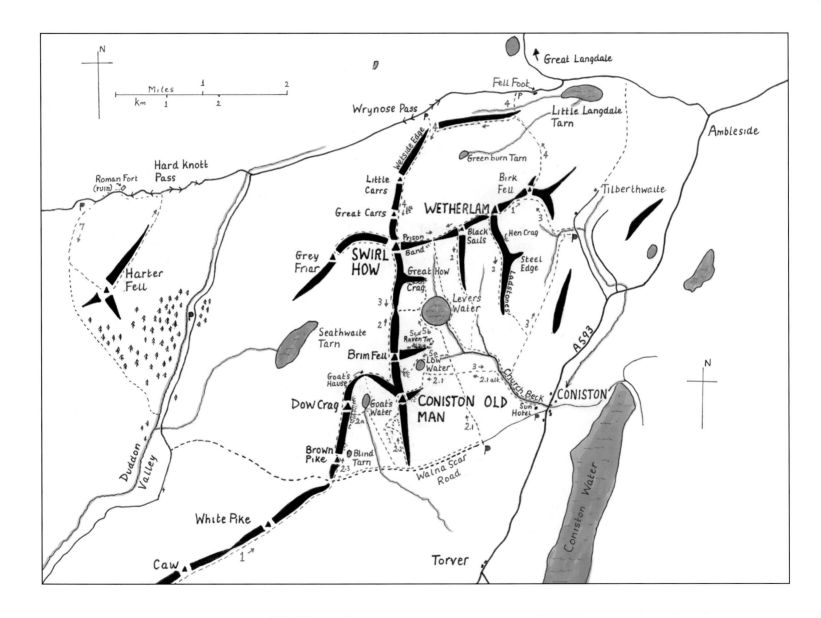

THE CONISTON FELLS

	Approximate Time	Star Rating	Assessment of Difficulty
1. Traverse of the Caw to Dow Crag Ridge and to Tilberthwaite	6–7 hours	**	—
2. Coniston Old Man to Wetherlam	5–6 hours	***	—
2.1 Coniston Old Man via East Face Quarries	1–2 hours	—	—
2a. Alternative scramble via Easy Terrace and the top of B Butttress	add 1/2–1 hours	***	2–3
2.2 Coniston Old Man via South Ridge	1–2 hours	—	—
2.3 Coniston Old Man via Brown Pike and Dow Crag	11/2–21/2 hours	**	—
3. Wetherlam to Coniston Old Man from Tilberthwaite	5–7 hours	**	—
4. Swirl How from Wetside Edge or Little Langdale	31/2–5 hours	*	—
5. Alternative scrambles to the tops			
5a. By Low Water Beck and Brim Fell to Coniston Old Man	11/2–2 hours	**	3
5b. Via Great How Crag to the main ridge	1–11/2 hours	*	2
5c. Via Raven Tor to Brim Fell	?	*	2
6. The Three Counties Walk	8–14 hours	***	—
7. Harter Fell from Eskdale	3–4 hours	*	—

THE CONISTON FELLS

The lower part of the Coppermines Valley, with its slag heaps and quarries, is not very attractive at all, but it is a most interesting place, as I first realised when I spent a fascinating day exploring some of the old mine workings. Some of the mineshafts go hundreds of yards under Levers Water and one can only speculate what sort of life miners must have led a hundred years ago, balanced precariously on planks, with candle lanterns, bridging huge drops in the black darkness. All the time there must have been the steady thumping noise of the great water-driven engines pumping out the water which continually poured into the

workings and perpetually dripped on to the toiling miners. The remains of the conduits that provided both the power to turn the pumps and to carry away the flood-water are still clearly visible, as are the 'iron pigs' that remain from the primitive smelting operations.

However, as you walk up the valley, this old industrial site is soon left behind and, from a fell-walker's point of view, the higher the better. One of the undoubted attractions of the group of peaks making up the Coniston fells is that it is possible to enjoy several high-level walks of five or six hours' duration at an altitude of around two thousand feet or more with splendid distant views over Coniston Water and, if the visibility is good, across to the peaks of Scafell, Scafell Pike and the Langdale Pikes.

The obvious centre for walking is Coniston village and from there, Church Beck, with good paths up either side, leads up the Coppermines Valley into the heart of the range. This is the approach for many of the scrambles on these fells but most of the best walks attain the peaks via the ridges. Let us start with a ridge traverse, which, although it is quite a long one, covers some rarely visited fells and almost all the best peaks in the group.

1. Traverse of the Caw to Dow Crag Ridge and to Tilberthwaite

The Coniston fells consist essentially of two ridges and this walk goes along the length of one of them and takes in most of the other. Although it is rarely done in this form, it is nevertheless a fine outing. As always with a traverse – as opposed to a round – there is a transport problem to be solved, but Caw is clearly visible from the secondary road to its west and after a field-track you are soon on the open fell. In this early section the way is over heather, grass and bracken and is virtually untracked, except by sheep. Not until you approach Brown Pike are you on obvious paths, but from then on you are on the edge of much steeper ground, culminating in Dow Crag summit.

Approaching and leaving Dow Crag there are dramatic views to Goats Water, seen far below down the great gullies that separate the five main buttresses, and across to the gentler slopes of Coniston Old Man. After Dow the path descends gently to Goats Hause, where one path descends past Goats Water while another rises back rightwards towards the Old Man. On a hot day very welcome running water can be found only a little way below the

hause where the stream that flows down to Seathwaite Reservoir suddenly wells up out of the ground in a clump of green moss.

You may, of course, return to Coniston village or Torver from here but to continue the walk make a rising traverse north-eastwards, bypassing the summit of the Old Man, to pick up an increasingly obvious path that heads for a point just below the summit of Brim Fell. There you will join the path along the main ridge, with a short descent and then a climb up to the jutting rocks of Great How, before the last nearly-level section to Swirl How's summit. Ahead is the long descent of the curiously-named Prison Band, but there is a good path down it to keep you on the straight and narrow and the objective is the fine peak of Wetherlam, dominating Little Langdale and with distant views to the Langdale Pikes and the Helvellyn range.

It is a steady climb, but the last of the day, for the descent is best down the rough and rocky but well-marked Wetherlam Edge, above Greenburn, to Birks Fell. Finally, you will go down the winding track high above the tumbling stream, the waterfalls and the disused quarries almost hidden in the fellside, to emerge by the hamlet of Low Tilberthwaite.

2. Coniston Old Man to Wetherlam – with three alternative approaches to the Old Man

The second very enjoyable walk – and a round – that can include virtually every peak in the group, is to tramp the ridge from Coniston Old Man to Swirl How (with an optional diversion to Grey Friar), and then go on to Black Sails and Wetherlam, before returning to Coniston. There are three main alternative approaches to the Old Man and this fine ridge.

2.1 Coniston Old Man via East Face Quarries

This is possibly the most popular, probably the fastest, and certainly the worst way. From Coniston on the right-hand side of Church Beck there is a metalled track into the Coppermines Valley, which is officially closed to cars, apart from access to the cottages, but this is better as a direct way towards Levers Water and the walks and scrambles in the upper part of the valley. So if starting from Coniston village, it is best to follow the path signed for the Old Man at the side of the Sun Hotel, which leads pleasantly up the left side of Church Beck, then by fields and stiles to the track at the bottom of the East Face quarries. Alternatively you may walk up the steep road beside the Sun Hotel – signed to the Walna Scar road farther on – and at the top of the first steep rise is a signed path over fields, ford and track towards the quarries. The last choice is nearly everybody's, which is to park at the end of the tarmac, beyond the fell gate, at the beginning of the Walna Scar road (GR 289971) then walk along the almost level track towards the quarries.

Whichever path you take, the aim is to get to the end of the quarry track then take the left fork upwards, grinding in low gear up the eroded way, avoiding the slithery slate and rusted cables that litter the track near the old slate-workings just below Low Water. After those pleasures you can enjoy the delights of the trudge up the zigzags to the ridge above and to the west (left) of Low Water, with a final and thankful last pull up to the summit cairn. This way up the Old Man is really much better as a descent, when you can dash quickly past ascending, and perspiring, parties. However, its popularity seems to remain unchanged.

It is worth mentioning that the continuation of the level track, beyond the point where the climb begins up to Low Water and the Old Man's summit, is probably the easiest approach to Levers Water and the scrambles on Great How and Little How.

2a. Alternative scramble via Easy Terrace and the top of B Buttress

For those with rock-climbing or reasonably wide scrambling experience – for this technically easy way is exposed in the upper section – there is an entertaining route directly up the great cliff of Dow Crag. Going south-west along Walna Scar Road, turn right after the third rocky gateway, climb the rise and follow the track towards Goats Water, with Dow Crag clearly visible ahead.

On reaching Goats Water, flat rocks enable you to ford the stream issuing from the tarn, then climb the path that leads to the mountain rescue box at the foot of the crag. When your tongue is hanging out you'll almost invariably find at least a trickle of clear water near the foot of the gully and only fifty yards or so to the right of the rescue box. This box is at the foot of B Buttress – the buttresses are all named alphabetically from left to right as you face the crag – and if you head up the rubble at its foot you will reach a very steep and black cleft (Great Gully) separating A and B buttresses. Left

again, beyond the steep rocks of A Buttress is another gully (Easy Gully) which is the rock-climbers' descent route. It is full of loose rock, and not a very inviting way of ascent for that reason.

However, there is a much more interesting way up, comparable to the traverse of Jack's Rake on Pavey Ark in Langdale, though this line is more exposed. It ferrets an easy, though airy, way up the main crag and in its lower part is the normal descent for climbers coming down from routes on B and C buttresses. Hands as well as feet are needed, but the holds are substantial, and as long as you don't suffer from vertigo you should have no problems. The object is to find the easiest way up, not the most difficult.

To make certain that you are on the right route, scramble towards A Buttress, which is the last main bastion of clean rock soaring 500 feet above the left-hand end of the crag. The route then initially goes up a shallow gully slanting back right across the face of B Buttress. After about 70 feet, the gully narrows to an extent which will give a fat person some pain, but it is fairly easily bypassed by holds on the right wall.

A little higher a distinct and level path is reached, running horizontally round the buttress, which looks as if it is clearly 'the way'. Do *not* be misled. The path has been worn by the feet of climbers who finish their climbs at this level. Consequently the path in front ends abruptly above fierce crags. Your way is to go slanting upwards in the line of the gully up which you first started, though you may also just as successfully head back slightly left and upwards too. As you go higher the little ledges lead left and right and left again, but always sensationally upwards. Fairly abruptly you are on the top of the buttress, which is connected to the rest of the mountain by a short ridge, so it is a very good viewpoint as well. It is a splendid way to get safely and exhilaratingly up one of Lakeland's great crags.

I went that way once when there was not a single climber to be seen and I climbed up with the more timid of my dogs in my rucksack, while the other scrambled up with me – with a judicious push here and there – to encourage him. He was normally a very good climber, but on this occasion he took a rush at a short wall in front of me and to my horror failed to find footholds above. He tipped off backwards, hurtled through the air and I felt certain that it would be the end of him. To my immense relief he hit a grassy ledge, shook himself, and

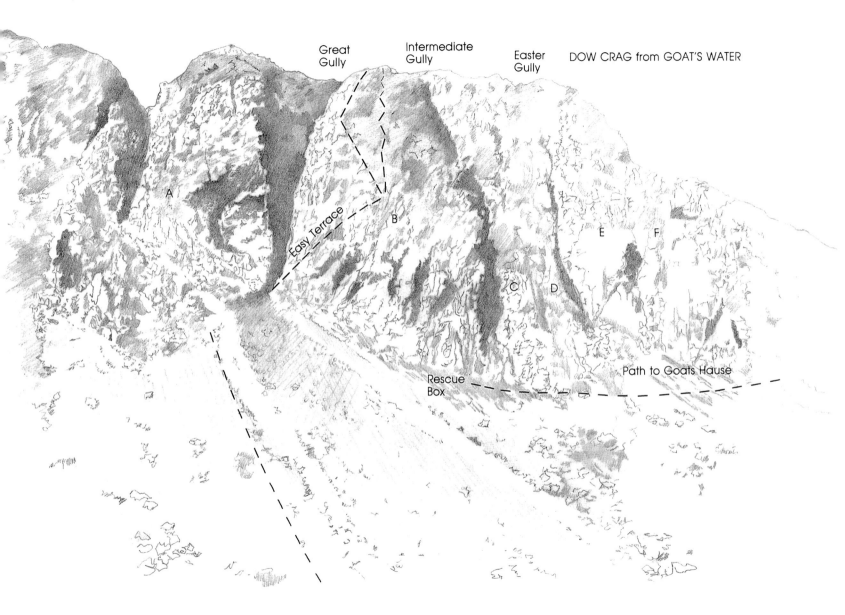

Great Gully

Intermediate Gully

Easter Gully

DOW CRAG from GOAT'S WATER

A

Easy Terrace

B

E

F

C

D

Rescue Box

Path to Goats Hause

immediately came back up to me, apparently unhurt. We carried on upwards, but I noticed that he kept much closer and when there were more little rock walls he cocked his head on one side and looked at me quizzically before jumping up them. However, by the time we had descended to Goats Hause and surmounted the Old Man, he was rushing around with just as much energy as ever.

By whichever way you achieve the summit of the Old Man, the continuation of this walk is along the broad ridge and over the top of Brim Fell. Then there is a short descent followed by the climb up to Great How – often mistaken for Swirl How – and finally the almost level stretch to Swirl How itself. The views to the Scafells and Langdale Pikes should get much better and if it is really clear it is well worth while walking the short distance to Grey Friar and back again purely for the views towards the Scafell range.

You are at the end of the main ridge and from Swirl How summit there is a choice of routes back to Coniston. Many walkers descend the curiously-named Prison Band ridge, which is a good way to go, and then descend straight down the line of Swirl Hawse Beck to the Coppermines Valley. I personally prefer to climb up to the high point of Black Sails and then down the delightful south ridge with its little rocky outcrops before descending into the valley. As a last choice you can continue beyond Black Sails to the summit of Wetherlam and then go down its south ridge, called Ladstones, and so back to Coniston. This gives the longest day in this direction, but you do stay on the high ridge until the last possible minute before the descent back to civilisation.

2.2 Coniston Old Man via the South Ridge

This is a much more enjoyable way, though apparently less direct. Go up the Walna Scar track, through the fell gate and, about a quarter of a mile farther on, heading up the south flank on the right is another quarry track. Just to the left of this a green pathway, not particularly used but well-cairned, climbs up the fellside towards the quarries. It makes a wide detour to avoid the workings then rises steadily with wide-ranging views across Coniston Water, eventually emerging on the shoulder of the Old Man just below the summit. You can then enjoy the view down to Low Water and across the Brim Fell ridge to Levers Water without having had to endure any of that toil up the eroded scree below.

2.3 Coniston Old Man via Brown Pike and Dow Crag

This is certainly the longest but possibly the most enjoyable approach to Coniston Old Man. Go up the steep road beyond the Sun Hotel to the fell gate and a little farther on the Walna Scar road to park, then walk along through three little rocky clefts until the path forks. Keep to the main track, the left fork, which rises very gently across the moor, then ascend more steeply to the pass over to the Duddon Valley. It is an interesting diversion to follow the green track leading off to the right just before reaching Brown Pike. This leads to some old mine-workings just above Blind Tarn, where there is still a complete and fully-roofed workman's shelter hidden in the slate spoil-heaps. It does seem though to have been built more for dwarfs to creep into than for men.

From Brown Pike it is an exhilarating walk along the edge of the cirque, with dramatic views down the great gullies, across to the slopes of the Old Man and so to the summit of Dow Crag itself. Now follows the steady descent to Goats Hause and the slanting path back right to Coniston Old Man.

3. Wetherlam to Coniston Old Man from Tilberthwaite

This is a really good day's walk but it is a bit tougher than many because it involves a climb at the end of the day. Leave your transport in one of the obvious car parks just below Low Tilberthwaite hamlet on the left-hand side of the beck. Shoulder your pack and head generally west up good footpaths, past the waterfalls down in the gill below and over the boggy ground to the east of Wetherlam's summit. There are various tempting ridges going up towards the peak, but the path curves round the rocky bluff of Hawk Rigg before heading west over Birk Fell to Wetherlam Edge. A series of rocky steps up this leads to the fine summit with its distant views down to Windermere and over to those marvellous jutting Pikes that draw the eye from almost every direction.

From Wetherlam's summit it is the main ridge in reverse: Prison Band, Swirl How, Brim Fell and the Old Man. The sting is in the tail, for, after the rapid descent down the quarry paths to Church Beck, you must then climb back from just north of the old workings to pick up the track heading east of Wetherlam's south ridge, and that track takes you back, tired but contented, along pleasant paths, to Tilberthwaite.

Wetherlam seen from Swirl How.

4. Swirl How from Wetside Edge or Little Langdale

The northern approach to the Coniston fells is either from Little Langdale up Greenburn – a rather dull approach which can, however, be enlivened by a scramble on the rocks of Great Carrs, for there are a couple of reasonably compact buttresses. Or, much more commonly, since few walkers can resist the temptation to park their cars as high up the road as possible, from the Three Shire Stone at the top of Wrynose Pass. From there the path climbs steeply to reach Wetside Edge, curves up to Great Carrs and Swirl How, and so along the main ridge to the Old Man. My own preference is the 'Greenburn Round'. Park just a little way up the Wrynose Pass road from Fell Foot, and then cross the stream where it runs through a boggy hollow below the wall-end. After a steep but short climb up the bracken covered slope opposite you will reach the path on the lower part of the ridge of Wetside Edge. With this start, the possibilities for the day's walking widen a little, especially since you retain the option of going over to Wetherlam from Swirl How and can descend into Greenburn towards Fell Foot from either end of Birk Fell. This may not sound much, but it means that you can return to your starting point without having to tramp back up Wrynose Pass.

On the edge of the Coniston fells is an extraordinary hole in the ground known as Hodge Close Quarry, which may be approached up the track on the other side of the stream from that by which you approach Tilberthwaite. On dry days its rock walls provide low-level and very accessible climbing for the experts and the quarry is also a haunt for aqua-divers. The narrow road up to the huge open area at the top of the quarry is well worth travelling on a clear day to enjoy yet another unexpected view across to the Langdale Pikes.

Coniston Fells from the Duddon Valley

Most mountain groups have their interesting and uninteresting sides, and it is unquestionably true that, although the wooded valley of the Duddon (Dunnerdale) is itself very attractive indeed, it gives a dull approach to the Coniston fells. There is absolutely no hint from this north-west side of the existence of the mighty Dow Crag, for instance, and the dusty Water Authority track to Seathwaite Reservoir is a weary trudge, even if you ignore the 'Private' signs (as most do). The Walna Scar road is probably the best approach if you do start from Duddon Valley, and the sign to look out for from the main road, about half a mile east of Seathwaite village, is that indicating 'Coniston, Unfit for Cars' – which is certainly true. Half a dozen cars can park nicely just beyond the last gate, and then the Walna Scar track leads obviously up the long slope of the fell and so to Brown Pike and the Dow Crag ridge.

5. Alternative scrambles to the tops
5a. Scramble via Low Water Beck and Brim Fell to Coniston Old Man

For the scrambler or mountain-walker looking for something a bit more exciting than usual, these fells do have a good choice of possibilities, apart from the scrambles on Dow Crag and Great Carrs already mentioned. For instance, Low Water Beck, the stream flowing from Low Water below the summit of Coniston Old Man, can provide an exciting hour or two. In its lower section the beck pours down a gully cutting through steep slabs and a direct ascent is not feasible for scramblers, so ways have to be found to bypass it. The nearer you stay to the cascade the more you will have to use roots and grass as hand-holds so a fairly wide sweep to the right is advisable before returning to the stream-bed as the angle of the rocks eases. From there it is delightful scrambling up the clean slabs on the right of the stream towards a deep V-shaped groove down which the water rushes. The groove can be avoided on the left, but don't fail to return to the watercourse for a last enjoyable few feet on an excellent slab just above the groove. Quite suddenly it all becomes much easier – and there is Low Water.

From Low Water there is the possibility of continuing this unusual alternative approach to Coniston Old Man by an excellent scramble to the top of Brim Fell. Circle the tarn to where a small stream flows into it, go up its right-hand side to where it splashes next to slabby rocks, then start scrambling up these on good holds until the angle eases. Easier ground follows to a short rock barrier, which is easily overcome by a little gully, then head for the lowest point on the rocks of the rather broken upper buttress ahead. A steep start up spiky holds leads to excellent slabs for some way and to a final buttress barred by a higher rock wall. To avoid this go into the gully on the left, which can be climbed for a few feet, until it becomes easier to scramble up the rocks on the right and so back above the steep bit. The summit ridge is then very near, with its cairn, and it is an easy walk along the ridge to the trig point and cairn on the top of the Old Man.

5b. Scramble via Great How Crag to the main ridge

Beyond the combe of Coniston Old Man and Brim Fell, in which lies Low Water, there is a greater cirque with Levers Water in its basin. Great How is the rocky point on the main ridge from Coniston Old Man to Swirl How and it is reached just before Swirl How. From that point an easy-angled spur ending in steeper crags runs roughly towards Levers Water and forms the boundary of the combe. This excellent scramble is on the left flank of the crags at the end of the spur and the best approach is consequently along the left side of Levers Water, either from the Coppermines Valley or from the east face quarries track.

Walking along this left side of Levers Water into the combe the crags of Little How are evident straight ahead, with Thunder Slab split by a distinctive curved crack. (There is, incidentally, a worthwhile scramble here for connoisseurs.) Farther right are the crags of Great How, with its left flank in view where this scramble lies. After crossing the beck, up which a footpath leads into the combe to join the main ridge, slant upwards on grass just below the boulders beneath Little How and Great How. When you have reached the right point you will be at an easy-angled spur of slabs well to the left end of the main crags, which is where the scramble starts.

To be certain of your starting place, as you look down to Levers Water a square roofless stone ruin will be visible below and slightly to the right and there is a cairn at the foot of the spur as well. From that angle you may see another stone building without a roof, a little higher up the slope than the ruin and farther left. This is curiously small and circular, reminiscent of the 'beehive' stone huts to be found in southern Ireland. It is reputed that this is a trap for foxes, a goose-bield – so called because it was baited with a dead goose. It is in a state of excellent preservation. It could be centuries old; after all German miners were prospecting this area in Tudor times.

For the scramble start up the easy slabs of the spur to a barrier of much steeper rock that must be circumvented. To the right looks like rock-climbing country, but at the left-hand end of the barrier is a short ledge under a rock roof. Getting on to the ledge is a little awkward but it leads immediately into a gully with good holds up its right wall and so to a wide grassy ledge above the difficulties. This ledge leads rightwards below a large slab into an easy-angled corner and so to much easier rocks above. Soon it is easy scramble-walking along the crest of the spur to finish up a path on to Great How's summit and the main ridge. This path is, I think, the result of walkers reaching Great How from the Old Man via Brim Fell and, thinking they have reached Swirl How, they set off down this path, realise their mistake and so reverse their steps. I hope so.

5c. Scramble via Raven Tor to Brim Fell

The east ridge of Brim Fell ends abruptly in the great rock prow of Raven Tor on its northern flank. It is seen very clearly from Levers Water but not visible from the normal approaches to these fells, which is perhaps why I overlooked it myself for many years. The crags appear to consist of many apparently disconnected slaty slabs, explaining their lack of interest to rock-climbers. However, leaving the footpath on the west side of Levers Water for a plod up steep grassy slopes below the crag to a point at its upper end, just before reaching a wide and uninviting gully, has its reward. A continuous rib of rock is revealed stretching upwards, initially at an easy angle; this is the key. It leads easily to ledges and slabs, steepens to more slabs and more ledges, trending towards points overlooking the gully, then back again. There is no one obvious route – and it is the better for that. It's a great way – and probably 400 feet long – to the top of Raven Tor, with easy ground beyond to Brim Fell.

6. The Three Counties Walk

This fine walk is obviously not limited by the bounds of the Coniston fells but, since it does include Coniston Old Man, this is as appropriate a chapter as any to mention it. It is really a 'mountain marathon' going over the highest points of land in 'old' Lancashire, Cumberland and Westmorland, which are Coniston Old Man, Scafell Pike and Helvellyn. The creation of 'Cumbria' robbed Lancashire of its finest mountains but the disappearance of Cumberland and Westmorland from the administrative vocabulary has not removed them from the affections of fell-walkers and climbers. This walk will recall nostalgic memories for many fell-walkers, but fitness and determination are necessary, for it is over about thirty-six miles of rough mountain terrain.

Start in Elterwater village in the early hours of the morning so that the walk along the road of Little Langdale towards Wrynose Pass is completed

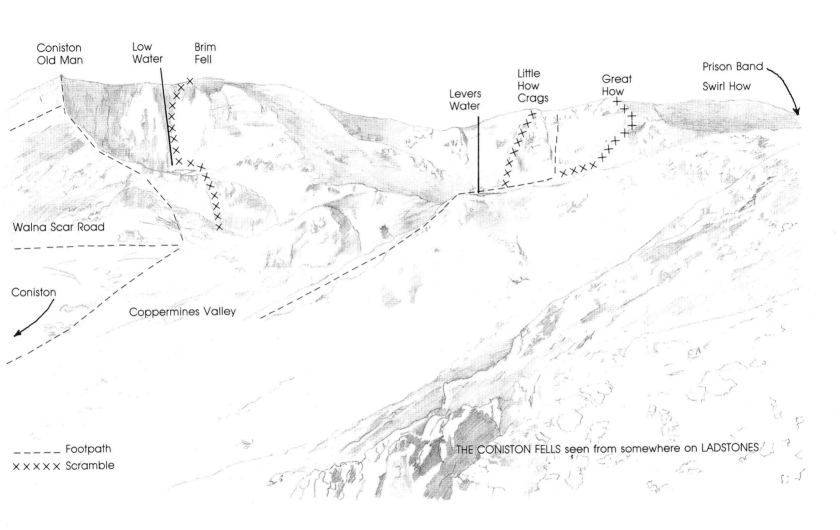

Coniston
Old Man

Low
Water

Brim
Fell

Levers
Water

Little
How
Crags

Great
How

Prison Band

Swirl How

Walna Scar Road

Coniston

Coppermines Valley

THE CONISTON FELLS seen from somewhere on LADSTONES

– – – – Footpath
× × × × Scramble

while it is traffic-free. Then it is up via Wetside Edge to Swirl How and the main ridge to Coniston Old Man to gain the first main summit. It is then necessary to reverse the route towards Swirl How and make for the hause between this and Grey Friar. Then, leaving footpaths behind for a while, strike down the fellside to Cockley Beck. The next objective is Scafell Pike, reached via Mosedale and Upper Eskdale, Cam Spout and Mickledore Ridge.

Leaving England's highest point behind, walk over the rough boulders to Esk Hause and then by good paths to Angle Tarn and the top of Stake Pass. Try to keep your feet dry on this section, over the moor to High Raise and then down Wythburn to the road at the bottom of Dunmail Raise. Helvellyn is ahead, and is reached via the path from Wythburn. The descent from this final summit is down Tongue Gill to Grasmere and a last weary but contented tramp over Red Bank back to Elterwater. A gruelling day and obviously not one for the faint-hearted, but it is a memorable experience.

7. Harter Fell from Eskdale

This Harter Fell is by no means one of the highest of the Lakeland fells, but it is difficult to ignore since it is a shapely little peak and it lies midway between the Scafells and the Coniston fells. It was one of the first Lakeland peaks that I climbed and I recall sitting in the Youth Hostel at Troutal in the Duddon Valley with my school friend and deciding that it would give us a much better day's walking if we included Harter Fell on our way to climb Slight Side and Scafell. Such is the ignorance – or presumption – of youth! We were very weary indeed when we trudged back over Hardknott Pass much later that night.

The Duddon Valley is very pretty but it is Forestry Commission country and the regimented conifers are very evident at the lower altitudes. The best circular route to the top of Harter Fell is from Eskdale. Furthermore, because this side is so rocky, there are scrambling alternatives to be found by the more adventurous.

Park at the bottom of Hardknott Pass on the Eskdale side, just uphill of the cattle grid, then cross the stream by a packhorse bridge and follow the path to the south-west. This is the start of a bridle-path that continues over the boggy moor to link up with Grassguards Gill and the Duddon. As height is gained the walker's path for Harter Fell veers off leftwards and it is a straightforward walk then to the three splendid rock tors on its summit.

However, the main pyramid of rocks is separated from the moor by a wide grassy shelf and if you walk left along this, rather than staying on the footpath, several scrambling ways can be worked out on the little crags along this section. Precise descriptions are both difficult and superfluous here; if you feel in the mood for a scramble you can surely find one on this intricate little mountain.

On one visit I had a strange sight. As I reached the summit I spotted a curious black cone on a tripod, with a separate aerial behind it, perched on the summit rocks. The owner of this equipment was huddled in a rocky corner and it transpired that he was an amateur radio enthusiast involved in a contest using ultra-high frequency waves which apparently only work as long as there is a direct line of sight between receiver and transmitter. As I watched and listened I realised that the operator was talking to somebody on Axe Edge in Derbyshire and he told me that he had spoken earlier to another contestant on the Welsh mountains. He had carried about seventy pounds of equipment up there for the day on the (quite correct) assumption that disturbances would be far fewer than on Coniston Old Man.

To descend, follow the path back to the top of Hardknott Pass – it is cairned, marked and boggy in places, particularly as you draw near to the timber, but it is easy going. Then shadow the road, avoiding the tarmac, of course, and have an exploratory look at the remains of the Roman fort just a few hundred yards uphill from where you left your transport three hours or so earlier. They are in a remarkably good state of preservation and the visit will provide a thoughtful finish to an interesting day.

Left: Low Water from the top of the East Face track of Coniston Old Man.
Overleaf left: From Green Crag to Harter Fell, Upper Eskdale.
Overleaf right: From Maiden Moor to Scope End and Robinson.

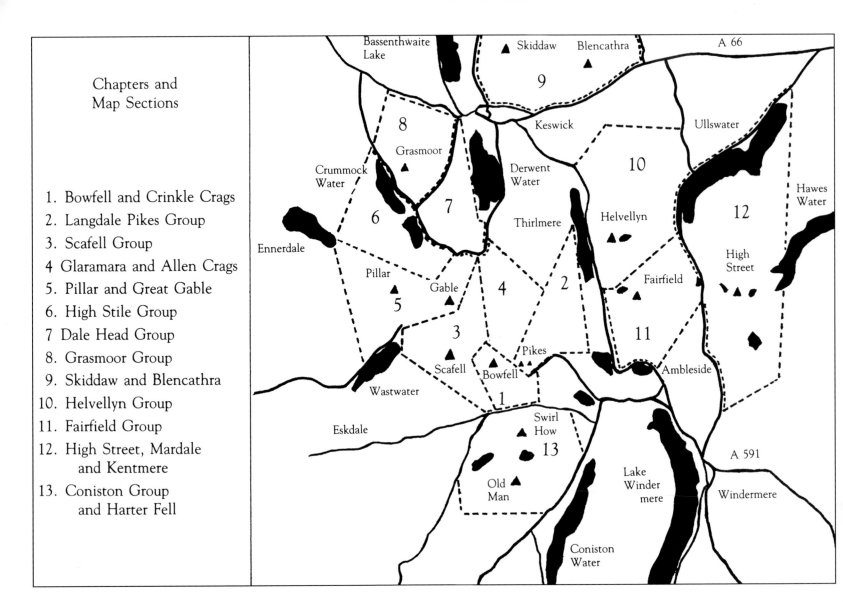

Chapters and
Map Sections